LAUREL
BEFORE HARDY

D1555878

LAUREL
BEFORE HARDY

Jenny Owen-Pawson and Bill Mouland

ISBN No. 902272 51 9

First published June 1984.
Designed by Fern Art, Kendal.
© Jenny Owen-Pawson and Bill Mouland
Typeset in 11pt Times Roman
Printed and Published in England by
Westmorland Gazette, Kendal.

To Nancy

Without whose help it would not have been possible to trace the life of Young Stan, and with grateful thanks for letting us publish treasured pictures from her album, and recalling for us the stories of the great comedian and his family which helped us build this picture of his early life.

Foreword

Co-operating with Jenny Owen-Pawson and Bill Mouland in the writing of this book has given me great pleasure. It has brought back the happy memories of Laurel and Hardy's tour of this country and Stan's reunion with his family, which I personally witnessed. His affection for his family and his pleasure in reminiscing with them over their young days was left in no doubt. He was brought up in a close and all embracing family and the memories of Ulverston were a never ending delight. Jenny Owen-Pawson and Bill Mouland's search for the truth has been particularly pleasing and I hope the following pages will reveal a part of Stan Laurel's life previously not known — his roots.

Nancy Wardell.

Contents

Acknowledgements

Mrs. Nancy Wardell.
Newcastle Central Library.
The Mitchell Library, Glasgow.
North Tyneside Library.
Mr. Bill Cubin, owner of the Laurel and Hardy Museum, Ulverston.
John and Marie Land.
Mr. John Garbutt.
Mr. John Marsh.
Mrs. Mabel Radcliffe.
Furness Holiday Guide.
Mr. John Lovelace.
The North West Evening Mail.
P. J. Mannex — Topography of Furness.
Stan Laurel by John McCabe.
Stan by Fred Lawrence Guiles.

Stan Laurel

849 OCEAN AVENUE
SANTA MONICA, CALIF.
Sept.25th.'59.

Dear Mrs Short:

       Thanks your nice letter,13th.inst.
Nice to hear from you again,& to know alls well & happy with
you.
   Many thanks for your kind birthday greetings - I was 69
last June.
   Yes, I was born in Ulverston,Lancs.in 1890. but left there at
an early age - lived in Bishop Auckland,Durham,a few years
then came to North Shields & went to school in Tynemouth.
My only connection with Jarrow was, that my Dad ran the
Theatre Royal there.
   Everything with me is just as usual,so not much to tell
you,so you will have to excuse my briefness. Thanks again
for your kind thoughts & sentiments - wish you & Mr Short
continued good health & happiness.
              Sincerely always:

                    Stan Laurel.
                   ─────────────
                    Stan Laurel.

Introduction

In the year that many of Stan and Ollie's fans will travel to Ulverston for the International Convention of the Sons of the Desert we have tried to paint this picture of Stan's young life in the town and across the Pennines where his family lived and he went to school. Many of the dates have faded in the mists of time as we have tried to piece together the movements of the family from Stan's birth in 1890 to 1910 when he finally left for fame and fortune in America.

Young Stan is a sketch of these times and is intended as a souvenir. We hope readers will visit some of the places illustrated in these pages and see for themselves the many that Stan cherished for the rest of his life. We have included a section of old photographs of Ulverston to try and show what the town looked like when Stan knew it well. Readers will still be able to find these places today and judge for themselves the changes that have taken place.

We owe a great debt of gratitude to Mrs. Nancy Wardell, who has helped us put this book together. Nancy's mother Mary Shaw was Stan's cousin. Mary and Stan were close friends in their early years and continued writing to each other after Stan settled in America. Through Mary's memories shared with her daughter Nancy we have been able to learn much of the family and have recounted many of the stories told about her famous cousin.

My Love & Fond
Thoughts Always
Mary & Herbert,
Affectionately —
Stan xx

Chapter 1

Young Laurel —
The Birth Of A Legend

Stan Laurel was, and still is, one of the world's best known and best loved comedians. Many would argue that he and his famous partner Oliver Hardy remain among the best in their field. For almost 20 years after Stan Laurel's death there is still a huge demand for his films, and a growing number of members of the Sons of the Desert, the fan club that has kept the legend of Laurel and Hardy strong across the world.

Much has been written of the two men with the gift to make people laugh through hundreds of films in almost as many countries even after their death. But little has been said of their early years. In the year that the International Convention of the Sons of the Desert is being held in Ulverston, the birth place of Stan Laurel, this is an attempt to tell the story of Laurel that has not been told; his first few years in Ulverston; the places he loved; the people he knew from his childhood, and those who probably helped to shape him into a great comedian.

His family was to remain important to him until the day he died. Even though he moved across the Atlantic, he wrote constantly to his sister, cousins and their children in the North of England. Through his correspondence, the warmth of his feelings for them and the

George and Sarah Metcalfe, taken long before the birth of Stan.

places he had known as a child shone brightly. He never failed to remember important dates back home and when he returned on tours to England he always made time for the family.

Stan Laurel was born Arthur Stanley Jefferson at Foundry Cottages, Ulverston, the home of his grandmother and grandfather on June 16, 1890. He was born in the small back bedroom of the two bedroomed terrace house in a quiet corner of the town. That house was to be his home for the first six or seven years of his life, and his grandmother, Sarah Metcalfe, was the one who looked after the little boy, who was always just "our Stan" to the family.

Sarah and her husband George came from Hawes in Yorkshire to settle in Ulverston in the mid-1800's. George probably came in search of work and set up a shoemaker's business in the town. Records show that he had a workshop in Newland Bottom, Ulverston, in the 1880's. The Metcalfes may well have been regarded with some suspicion by the people of the then Lancashire town (Ulverston became part of Cumbria in 1974) because they were "off-comers", a term still used for people not native to this part of the country. Nonetheless, they seem to have settled down happily in a little cottage in Oxford Street, later moving to 3, Foundry Cottages — a street named because it had a foundry at the end of it. It was renamed Argyle Street in the mid 1890's.

George and Sarah had two children, Margaret, always known as Madge, and Sarah, who was known as Auntie Nant to Stan and the rest of the family. Both were born in Ulverston and it was while Madge was singing with a choir in the town that she was admired by one Arthur Jefferson — later known universally as A. J. After but a glimpse of Madge, and without even having met her, Mr. Jefferson told his friends he would one day marry her!

A. J., who was to become a well-known actor, sketch writer and theatre manager of the day worked at The Gaff, a theatre in Argyle Street and he was not wrong in his bold prediction of marriage . . . on March 19, 1884 he married Madge Metcalfe in an Ulverston church. They did not remain in the town long, as Arthur's work took him all

*Stan and his
grandmother outside
the Metcalfe's house,
3 Argyle Street.*

Madge and A. J. Jefferson taken with grandma, Stan, Gordon and Beatrice,

The Shaws: Auntie Nant, Uncle John, Cousins Mary, Elsie, Nellie and John.

over the North of England. Madge adapted her own talents and turned her hand to acting, appearing in many of her husband's plays. But she returned to Ulverston, to her mother in Argyle Street to give birth to the son who was to become a household name across the world. Stan was the second of the Jefferson's four children. His elder brother Gordon, sister Beatrice and young brother Teddy, spent much of their time at Argyle street, although Stan was the only one of the children who actually lived with Grandma and Granda Metcalfe.

Stan's Auntie Nant also married and settled in Ulverston, not far from the Metcalfe family's home. Nant's husband, John Shaw, had come to the town to run the local co-operative store. His family came from Dewsbury, where they were rag merchants. They had six children, Mary, Elsie, Nellie, Jack, George and Charlie. Mary, just two years older than Stan, and Elsie, five months younger, were his closest playmates. Mary later settled in Yorkshire, where she married Herbert Jennings and had a daughter Nancy. Nancy remembers her mother, who died in 1970, talking of those early years in Ulverston.

Shortly after Stan's birth, Auntie Nant took young Mary across the fields to visit the new arrival. They nearly did not get to Argyle Street because Nant tripped in the mud and there were tears! Stan was not a healthy baby and the family feared he was not going to survive. The Metcalfes were strong Christians and Stan was quickly christened. But he did pull through those first difficult months and his birth was registered in August 1890. Perhaps it was because Stan had such a shaky beginning that he earned a special place in his grandmother's heart. It may also have been the reason why Stan was the only one of the Jefferson children to stay in Ulverston while the rest of the family travelled.

The Metcalfes were not wealthy and life must have been cramped when all the children were visiting, but it was always remembered as a happy home. When the children did get out of hand they were threatened with 'the wash house' by Granda, who by all accounts would stand no nonsense. If they were naughty they were made to sit out in a dark wash house in the back yard until they had learned to behave. It seems that Stan, growing up full of harmless boyish mischief, was the most frequent visitor there. Mary often wondered why he did not seem to mind being banished to the wash house when the others dreaded it. Later she discovered why . . . stashed away in the darkness were matches, candles and comics! It appears that Stan used the punishments to catch up on his reading!

Chapter Two
Early Mischief

Young Stan came to know the streets and shops of Ulverston well through shopping expeditions with his Grandma. They made a lasting impression on him for he later spoke in letters to England, of the narrow cobbled streets where he and Grandma went to buy family provisions. Occasionally he would be treated to his favourite treacle toffee. Stan was fascinated by the big plate glass windows of the town's shops and Mrs. Metcalfe would often find that she had left him behind as she walked. Retracing her footsteps she would catch him gazing through the glass, making faces. It would be nice to think that it was those shelves that first saw the famous cry baby face of Stan Laurel as he scratched the top of his tousled head.

It was not only Ulverston that Stan remembered in later life when writing from his home in Beverley Hills, California. His grandmother used to take the children on trips around the Lake District and into a countryside loved by the whole family. Years later, Stan's cousin, Mary Jennings sent him a holiday postcard and Stan wrote back of the fond memories the picture had brought him. "It reminded me very much of Lake Windermere," he said.

Most of the family excursions were by train. The Ulverston and Lancaster railway had arrived in the town 33 years before Stan's

THE REV. CANON AYRE, M.A.
VICAR OF HOLY TRINITY, ULVERSTON.

Atkinson Copyright

The Rev. L. R. Ayre married Stan's parents on March 19, 1884.

birth and the steam trains huffed and puffed close by the Metcalfe's Argyle Street home. It was on one of these outings that Stan showed cousin Mary just how far his mischief could take him. They were sitting in the train, gazing out across Morecambe Bay when Stan suddenly produced his grandfather's stirrup strap, obviously an object of some disciplinary significance in the Metcalfe household! To Mary's horror he flung it out of the window and into the sea. But all was in vain, because Granda had more than one stirrup strap, to supplement the sanction of banishing Stan to the wash house as punishment for some misdemeanour!

This is now the home of Mrs. Mabel Radcliffe and her husband Norman. A Miss Clarke and her mother moved to 3 Argyle Street in 1906 when the Metcalfe's left Ulverston. Miss Clarke died in 1977 and Mrs. Radcliffe bought the house with her previous husband Henry Allen. He died and she has now remarried. Mrs. Radcliffe has altered the house but it retains a plaque marking Stan's birthplace.

The washhouse, to the right, where Stan caught up on his reading. It remains much as it was in the Metcalfe's time.

Mary and Stan were not the only ones to enjoy the Lakeland excursions. There could have been at least half a dozen youngsters at a time on some of them, including Stan's elder brother Gordon, who later became a London theatre manager and rescued Stan when he returned penniless from a disastrous continental tour at the beginning of his career. Stan later repaid the debt, and took Gordon with him to America. Stan's sister, Beatrice Olga Jefferson, was born in December 1894 at South View, Bishop Auckland. She was also a talented actress and completed several tours of Ireland, but as Stan put it later: "She never made it big." After her marriage, Beatrice ran a pub for many years at Bottesford near Nottingham. She had a picture gallery of her famous brother and Oliver Hardy behind the bar. Stan's brother Teddy was born in April 1901 at North Shields in the family's Dockwray Square home. Stan took him to America as well where he became his chauffeur. Teddy died in 1933, allegedly as a result of dental treatment he had received earlier in the day. Records show that the Jeffersons also had another child, christened Sydney Everitt, who was born on April 30, 1899 at Dockwray Square. He died within months.

*Madge Metcalfe,
Stan's mother — a
picture taken in North
Shields.*

Family Tree

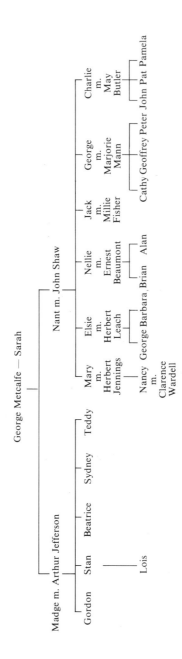

George Metcalfe — Sarah

Madge m. Arthur Jefferson   Nant m. John Shaw

Gordon   Stan   Beatrice   Sydney   Teddy

Lois

Mary m. Herbert Jennings

Nancy m. Clarence Wardell

Elsie m. Herbert Leach

George   Barbara   Brian   Alan

Nellie m. Ernest Beaumont

Jack m. Millie Fisher

George m. Marjorie Mann

Cathy   Geoffrey   Peter   John   Pat   Pamela

Charlie m. May Butler

Chapter Three
A Memory of Sawrey

The Ulverston connection began to fade before the turn of the century when Stan's Auntie Nant and Uncle John Shaw moved away from the town. For a while they lived a short way down the Furness railway line at Flookburgh where John Shaw managed another co-operative shop. The distance was nothing to the Metcalfes and Stan was a frequent visitor to the house in Flookburgh with his Grandma and Granda, and his friendship with playmates Mary and Elsie continued. The Shaws' next moved further into Lakeland where John went into business for himself taking over a grocery store at Sawrey, a village later to become famous through author Beatrix Potter.

In 1955, Stan wrote from California to Nancy Wardell in Dewsbury after she had told him of a holiday she had recently spent in Lakeland. He told her: "Your visit to the Lake District brought back to me many happy memories of my holidays there with your grandparents. I can see the old grocery shop and the apple orchard opposite very vividly when your mother, Jack, Charlie, Nellie and poor Elsie were all kids together and full of mischief."

He spoke of 'poor Elsie' as she had died, at the age of 39. It is ironic that Stan regarded his cousins as full of 'mischief' as they always claimed that he was the chief mischief maker and ring leader

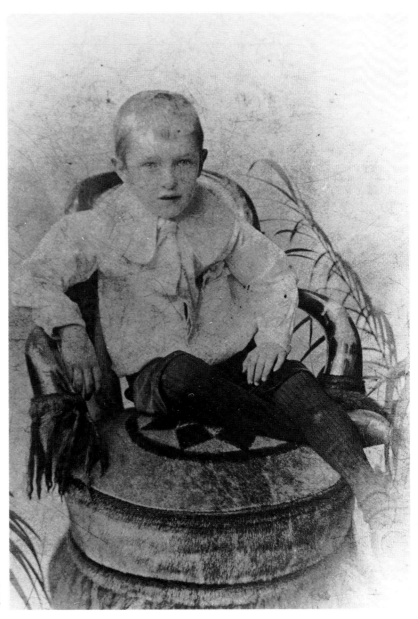

Stan sat for this picture
in North Shields
around 1897

Grocery shop, Sawrey, today.

The Apple Orchard, where Stan and his cousins played at Far Sawrey.

of the children! Mary Jennings later told Nancy how Stan would make her ride on the cross bar of his bicycle much to her trepidation and his amusement. He was the one who organised a children's theatre and made the others take parts in the plays, although Mary always preferred to stay behind the scenes, playing the piano. On that visit to Sawrey, in the 1950's, Nancy's father Herbert had sat down on a seat of wet paint. It appealed to Stan when he heard about it. He

Beatrice, Stan,
Granda, Grandma
and Teddy. Taken in
the backyard at
3 Argyle Street, to the
right is Stan's
washhouse.

probably thought it was a scene straight from one of his comedies. He wrote: "I got a good laugh re your Dad sitting on the fresh painted garden seat, I can just imagine his expression and your mother's. It must have been a scream." The apple orchard that Stan remembered so fondly is now only a shadow of its former days. But the grocery shop is still recognisable 80 years on from when Stan visited and played here. with his cousins.

At the beginning of the 1900's the Shaws and their children left Lakeland and moved to Batley where they settled in a large Victorian house in Warwick Road. In years to come the house became as familiar to Stan as the old grocery shop and the apple orchard.

Chapter Four

Captured for the Family Album

Thankfully Stan Laurel's family was always careful to keep photograph albums up to date as the early pictures reproduced on these pages show. Most of the family portraits in the Ulverston days were taken by Mr J. Hargreaves, a well known photographer of the area. He was known not only for his portraits but also pictures of local scenery. Not long before Stan was born he took pictures of Ulverston and Dalton-in-Furness which were to appear in the 'Holiday Resort Guide' of towns and villages on the Furness railway route. Stan, his brothers and sister and cousins were no strangers to Mr. Hargreaves' studio in Lightburn Road. He also had studios in Millom and Dalton, but his main work was done at Lightburn Road. A description of Mr. Hargreaves' shop appeared in the Holiday Guide, just as it would have been when Stan was taken there:

"Situated at the west end of the town and within a short distance of the railway station and post office facing the cattle market and drill hall and on the way to Conishead Priory. The establishment occupies a corner site in this central position and comprises a spacious and well furnished reception room in which may be inspected a large selection of choice examples of high class portraits, groups and views in every form of modern photography from the tiniest miniature to the handsome enlargements in carbon, platino-

Stan with his cousins Nellie and Elsie.

type and opal for which Mr. Hargreaves is so widely noted as an expert specialist."

The elaborate props and background which appear in all the photographs of the children bear witness to the fact that Mr. Hargreaves took great care with all his work. The Holiday Guide tells us: "The studio proper is a large and finely lighted apartment provided with a complete equipment of apparatus and accessories containing all the most up to date improvements conductive to successful operative work in all branches of the art."

3 Argyle Street as it was when the Metcalfe family lived there.

Stan's little sister
Beatrice, taken in
Ulverston.

*Stan's Cousins
Nellie, Mary, & Elsie
taken at Ulverston.*

The family also had its own photographer in Stan's elder brother Gordon. He took this photograph of Stan and his mother on January 29, 1904 outside their home in Dockwray Square, North Shields.

Chapter Five
A Town of Faded Fortune

When young Stan was not off on day trips there was plenty to amuse him at home in Ulverston both around the house in Argyle Street and further afield in the town. At home, one of the children's favourite past-times was dressing up and on fine days Stan and the others would play this in the back yard. They were fond too, of riding their bicycles, and in those days Grandma would not have worried much when they disappeared down the street together, because it was before the days of traffic rushing through the town and a by-pass which cut Ulverston in two.

Eight years before Stan's birth Mannex wrote in a topography of the Furness area: "This is a neat and well-built market town and port, delightfully situated on the Leven estuary and partly on the sides of gentle acclivities with a southern aspect and amidst an amphitheatre of hills open to the seaward." He said although the town was very old, it had been given a face lift and looked 'modern'. "It is still the mart for the agricultural productions of the district and was until late years the chief port for the shipment of the Furness ores. Though in commercial importance it has paled before the light of its youthful rival, Barrow, yet it is a wealthy and thriving town. This is evidenced by the various important trades and professions enumerated in its Directory, by the elegantly furnished shops which

Stan dressed up against the cold!!

*. . . And now my
profile.!*

View across the Bay to the Leven viaduct.

adorn the streets and by the magnitude and accommodation of its chief hotels". Mannex went on to tell his readers: "Ulverston has long been regarded as the key to the lakes and during the summer season a large amount of passenger traffic passes through the town on its way to Windermere."

Another of Stan's great loves was fishing in Ulverston's canal. It was a hobby he probably learnt very early in life from his uncle John Shaw and it was one of his favourite past-times. Stan did not have to go far to fish because the canal ran close to his home. His favourite spot was out beyond the old North Lonsdale Iron and Steel Company Limited, which is today the home of the Glaxo chemical industry. Behind him across the Bay, ran the viaduct carrying the railway down to Carnforth. Close to where Stan sat waiting for a bite on his line, was a pair of fine old lock gates. Many years later he wrote of swinging on them but sadly these have now virtually rotted away.

*Canal Foot where Stan
fished. In the distance
is the Hoad
Monument.*

The Ulverston Canal had been cut in 1794 almost 100 years
before Stan was born. It was one and a quarter miles long and
connected the town with the open sea. In 1882 Mannex wrote: "It is
said to be the shortest, straightest and deepest in England and is
navigable for vessels of 300 tons burthen, which can be moored in
safety in the capacious basin constructed for the purpose."

The lock gates as they look today.

In the early 1880's the canal was constantly in use carrying iron, copper ore, slate and gunpowder, but when the docks opened at Barrow, traffic on the canal stopped and its shipyards became deserted. A new pier, the Beaconsfield pier, was built by the North Lonsdale Iron and Steel Company. It ran out some way into the Bay and provided a place for steamers and other vessels to load and unload. "The pier is providing a source of great advantage not only to the company but also to the town, and it is hoped it may be the nucleus of other extensive works which may bring a revival of Ulverston's prosperity as a port," wrote Mannex 100 years ago. Sadly his hope was never to be realised and Ulverston's canal has been allowed to deteriorate over the years.

Chapter Six
A Lighthouse and a Monument

Stan well may have passed the town's cemetery on his fishing expeditions to the canal and it was here he saw something which he never forgot. It was a quaint, miniature lighthouse built in memory of Dr. Thomas Watkins Wilson who died in London in 1897, when Stan was seven. Dr. Wilson and his daughter Mary used to spend their holidays at Ulverston and when he died she wanted to leave something there in remembrance of him. The lighthouse, with an anchor sculpted around the base, had a light at the top which was once lit 24 hours a day. The gas pipe can still be seen running to the lamp high up on the stone memorial. Inscribed on the monument along with many lines of verse are the words: "Every year for 15 years we were wont to spend some months at Conishead Priory in remembrance whereof and in token of reverence and love this monument is here erected by his child Mary". Inscribed is Dr. Wilson's favourite poem.

Also carved is: "Thomas Watkins Wilson MD, born December 13, 1812 and brought up in Edinburgh, he passed his active life in India. After 19 months of suffering he fell asleep 20 minutes to 7 on Friday evening January 15, 1897 in London".

The light on the monument shone out constantly until the First

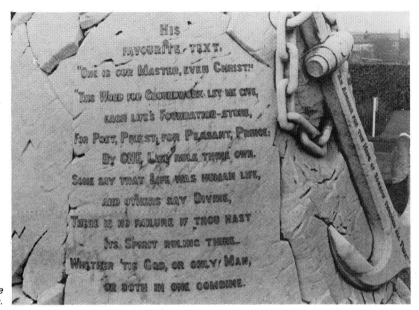

His
FAVOURITE TEXT.
"ONE IS OUR MASTER, EVEN CHRIST!"
THIS WORD FOR GUIDANCE LET ME GIVE,
EACH LIFE'S FOUNDATION-STONE,
FOR POET, PRIEST, FOR PEASANT, PRINCE;
BY ONE LAW RULE THINE OWN.
SOME SAY THAT LIFE WAS HUMAN LIFE,
AND OTHERS SAY DIVINE,
THERE IS NO FAILURE IF THOU HAST
ITS SPIRIT RULING THINE.
WHETHER 'TIS GOD, OR ONLY MAN,
OR BOTH IN ONE COMBINE.

Dr. Wilson's favourite poem.

World War when it was extinguished because of the black-out. It was lit again, until the Second World War when it was again extinguished, and sadly has never burned since, although the lighthouse remains.

South Lakeland Council agreed to relight the monument temporarily for the International Convention of the Sons of the Desert.

The monument and its light fascinated seven year old Stan Laurel. In 1932 he and a Daily Herald reporter were looking at Stan's name in lights above a theatre in London's Leicester Square . . . "Looks great but kind of wasteful," he told the reporter, "but you should see the lighthouse in the graveyard at Ulverston in Lancashire where I was born. They put it up when I was a kid, a tombstone with a light on top. It was the Eighth Wonder of the World to me. Ever since then it's been my ambition to have a tombstone like that."

*Lighthouse tombstone
in Ulverston Cemetery.*

The lighthouse was built by Mr. Thomas Affleck's firm of sculptors, monumental and general masons. The Holiday Guide mentioned Mr. Affleck's premises . . . "They are conveniently situated in Dragley Beck Lane, and comprise the usual structure and appliance for the business, the latest machinery being employed for sawing limestone etc. An excellent and thoroughly artistic display is made in the way of monumental sculpture the designs being in admirable taste and evincing a high degree of talent and accurate knowledge of the art on the part of the proprietor".

The Street where the children played in front of The Wesleyan School.

The street where Stan and his cousins played was overlooked by another monument — the Hoad Monument — on the hill above the town. It was erected 40 years before Stan's birth in memory of Sir John Barrow who was also born in Ulverston, at Dragley Beck. Stan's grandparents probably watched Hoad Monument being built high up above the town behind their home. But Stan remembered it for the great fun he and the others had there at Easter time when they painted eggs, climbed the hill and rolled them down the fell, a great old English tradition.

Hoad Monument stands unchanged since it was built more than 130 years ago and it is still possible to climb up the hill to it. The monument cost £1,250 and looks very much like the Eddystone Lighthouse. It was built of massive blocks of mountain limestone hewn out of the hillside close by. The top is reached by a flight of 112 steps where eight openings look out over the landscape.

32 Oxford Street, the first Ulverston home of Sarah and George Metcalfe.

Sir John Barrow's family was not wealthy and he went to the local Town Bank School. Later he went to work as a clerk in an iron founder's office in Liverpool. He studied maths and then went to Greenwich to teach. His first step in public life was as private secretary to Sir George Staunton and he travelled with him on an expedition of Lord MacCartney to China. On his return he wrote of his journeys and continued travelling and writing for many years. He was one of the main planners of an ill fated expedition to the Arctic in which Sir John Franklin died.

Sir John Barrow died on November 23, 1848, aged 85 years in London. Two years later, the people of Ulverston put up their memorial to one of the great men of the town. Only recently a school in Argyle Street has been named after him.

A Lighthouse and a Monument

Hoad monument taken in 1897 when the diamond jubilee bonfire was built beside it.

Chapter Seven

Ulverston and Treacle Toffee

Another familiar spot to young Stan was the railway station where many of his expeditions started, either to Flookburgh to visit the Shaws, or Lake Windermere with Grandma Metcalfe or his parents. The station is as impressive today as it was when Stan's family waited on the platforms for its trains. Recently it has been given a face-lift and the old canopies outside the station have been replaced in their original style. The first train steamed into Ulverston in 1857, but the station was rebuilt in the 1870's when it was described as "a light elegant structure and very conveniently arranged for the large amount of passenger traffic which passes through. The approaches are ornamented with shrubberies kept in beautiful order and the station is not less remarkable for the extreme neatness than for the cleanliness and order which everywhere prevail." The old seats at the station are of special interest. The original emblem of the old Furness Railway was a squirrel and the seats are each now engraved with the little animal as a reminder of the old days. Around the corner stands Holy Trinity church where Stan's mother and father were married in 1884. But times have changed and it is now probably the only church in the world to be converted to a sports centre! Stan would not recognise the road which runs beside it either. For Ulverston by-pass has been cut through the town beside the church. The Metcalfe family was religious and undoubtedly Stan

*Ulverston Station
with its restored
canopies.*

attended services here with them just before the turn of the century.
Holy Trinity was only 52 years old when the Jeffersons were married,
but three years before Madge and A. J. walked up the aisle it had been
restored and enlarged. One of the additions was a beautiful marble
reredos from the studios of Miles and Affleck, who built Stan's
eighth wonder of the world.

The Wesleyan Sunday School also formed an important part of
the family's life. Stan and his cousins certainly attended when they
lived just down the street.

Like most other boys Stan had a sweet tooth and a special treat
for him was a visit to Mr. Gillam's general store on a corner of
Market Street. The shop remains much as it was before the turn of
the century — its windows full of tempting food and the counters
piled high inside. Behind the counter you can still see the original old
fashioned drawers hiding more riches. The name has not changed
either, for serving behind the counter is Mr. Gillam working away as
his father and grandfather did before him. The beautiful old tin tea

Holy Trinity Church today with the by-pass running close by. In the distance is the Hoad Monument.

Mr. Gillam's shop, much the same inside today as it was when Stan knew it.

41

Original toffee tin.

caddies are still in everyday use and even the old toffee tin which contained Stan's favourite sweet is still there. In January 1950 writing to England from Paris he said: "I used to go shopping on Market Street with Grandma Metcalfe — that was a big treat for me. Beers Treacle toffee, it sure was good!" It was ironic that Stan should remember that sugary sweet then, for he was recovering from an operation in Paris. His weight had plummeted from 165 to 114 pounds. and he had learned shortly before his illness that he was a diabetic.

Mr. Gillam's general store.

Mr. Gillam's shop stands in the shadow of the town clock which has a face on all four sides and the date 1845 inscribed beneath each face. It has changed little since the beginning of the 1900's. But on one occasion in the late 1800's it needed some attention and legend has it that it was Granda Metcalfe who repaired it.

Ulverston's Coronation Hall had a special place in Stan's heart. He visited the town with Oliver Hardy for the last time in 1947 and it was as great an occasion for Stan as it was for the people who crowded around him. He was ceremonially handed a copy of his birth certificate and taken back to his birthplace. It brought back many happy memories and on his return to American he wrote to his cousin Mary in Dewsbury: "Funny you should mention Ulverston, we have just got back from visiting there today, quite a turnout — I was presented to the folks at the Coronation Hall and was given a copy of my birth certificate on the balcony outside, then went over to 3 Argyle Street, went through the old house, brought back many memories, had lunch with the officials at the golf club, a wonderful time, was thrilled to death."

Town clock.

Stan and Ollie in
Ulverston, 1947.

Stan's Aunt Nant,
Uncle John and
cousins all born at
Hartley Street.

Chapter Eight
Death of a Theatre

Stan did not have to go far to the theatre when he lived with his grandparents, for the Hippodrome was just across the road in Lightburn Park on the site of the newly named Sir John Barrow School. Stan's father and mother were players in the tent-like theatre known as Spencer's Gaff and A. J. was also manager in the early 1880's. The theatre was made of wood with a canvas roof, but later it was re-roofed and modernised under the managership of Arthur Denville. Sadly in 1910, the year that Stan left for America with the Fred Karno troupe, the theatre burnt down.

It had served a purpose for Stan's father, for he learned much from his days at the Gaff. Many of the Victorian melodramas he took with him had been enacted first on the boards of the Hippodrome. Ulverston fire brigade records for the night of the blaze show that the alarm was raised at 3.25 on the morning of April 3 and firemen did not return to their station until after 5 am. The account of the inferno appeared the next morning in the North West Daily Mail: "Ulverston was the scene of the most destructive fire experienced for many years," it said, "the large Hippodrome Theatre in Lightburn Park together with the whole of the scenery, properties, stage wardrobe etc being reduced to a blackened mass of ruins within an incredibly brief space of time."

*The Staff and
Orchestra at The Gaff.*

Site of Old Hippodrome in Argyle Street, now the home of Lightburn School.

The fire was discovered by lamplighter Mr. Isaac Lancaster who lived close by in Neville Street. The fire brigade and the manager — Mr. Denville, along with his wife who was the proprietress of the theatre, were quickly on the scene, but the North West Daily Mail reported: "The fire had travelled with such fierce rapidity that by this time the roof and the sides of the structure had collapsed and the interior was one mass of lurid flame, the powerful illumination from which created such a large glare in the sky as to attract crowds of spectators from far and near, but thanks to the efforts of the police the throng was prevented from hampering work of the firemen."

The firemen quickly realised that the theatre was a lost cause and concentrated their efforts on saving the carriage works of Messrs Wilson and Son nearby which was also in danger of catching fire. The newspaper reporter told his readers: "The flames from the falling debris having set light to the eaves of the showroom containing a number of finished and partly finished conveyances, and a quantity of motor tyres." The theatre which was only partly insured was lost forever and the cause of the blaze shrouded in mystery. On Saturday night a large audience in the theatre, which held 1,400 people, had watched 'Saved from the Sea'. Theories that the fire had been started by a cigarette carelessly thrown by a member of the audience were soon discarded. The paper tells us: "The theatre was fitted and equipped in the most up to date style with spacious pit, boxes, gallery, a roomy stage, with a fine proscenium, dressing rooms etc and it was lighted throughout by electricity, whilst the stock company, whose performances have been drawing very large audiences nightly since the middle of December last when the local justices granted Mr Denville a theatrical licence was admitted to be one to the best travelling in the provinces. In fact such good business was being done that the manager said he was fully expecting to prolong his stay in Ulverston beyond Whitsuntide."

Chapter Nine
Old Ulverston

On the next few pages we have tried to show the background to the life of young Stan Jefferson by reproducing some early pictures of the town where he spent his first few years. Stan was certainly familiar with the scenes in all these photographs for on countless occasions he accompanied his grandma when she went shopping. Ulverston consisted of four main streets and many smaller ones, Queen Street being the main road leading from the railway station, crossed by Market Street.

This was Market Place in 1897, as Stan would have remembered it. The shop on the right is still a Chemist's run by Hewitts. Further down the street to the left is the home of Ulverston's Laurel and Hardy Museum which is run by a keen fan Mr. Bill Cubin.

The canal locks at Ulverston as they were when Stan knew them and swung on them before the turn of the century.

The Great Gale of February 27, 1903.

Train crossing the Mail Train on the Leven Viaduct, near Ulverston, Furness Railway, overturned by the force of the gale in the early morning of the 27th Feb. 1903.

The Old Leven or Kent viaduct which carries the railway across Morecambe Bay to Ulverston. Before the railway was built the only way to get across the bay without making a massive diversion was by using a guide to lead the way over the treacherously shifting sands. The firm path was quite wide, however, once you found it and coaches easily made the crossing. Today the guide still exists, although only to lead parties of walkers and the sands still claim the unwitting. The viaduct itself was a spindly looking affair when Stan would have known it, but in 1916 its support columns were clad in the brickwork of today.

53

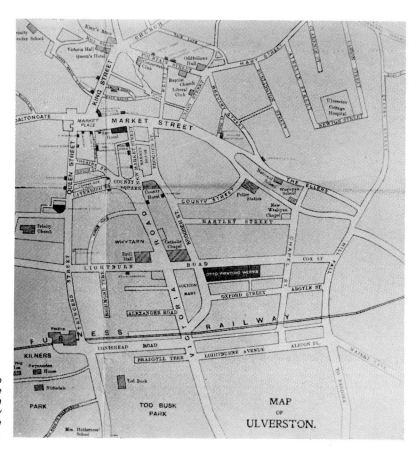

An 1879 Map showing Argyle Street and Ulverston town before the by pass separated the two.

The altar inside the
church where the
Jefferson's took their
vows. The window
remains but the
church has been
converted to a sports
centre.

As Stan descended Market Street from the Market Place with his grandmother he would have passed Mr. John Boulton's saddlery shop which had stocks of various saddles, harness bits and bridles hanging on display outside. The Sun Hotel, claiming to be the oldest in the town, was also said to be a favourite resting place for tourists. A brochure of the day said: "The tariff generally is on a most moderate scale, when the excellence of the accommodation is taken into account." Other shops in Market Street included tailor and draper Mr. Thomas Iddon whose premises were immediately opposite the Sun.

39842. ULVERSTON: MARKET STREET.

*Another view of
Market Street.*

Dr. Wilson's Monument taken in 1897 shortly after it was built.

Lower Market Street.

*The Wesleyan Church,
beside The School,
where Stan and his
cousins played.*

County Square.

Station Road.

Princess Street.

New Market Street

Chapter Ten
Families on the Move

During the first seven years of Stan's life, his father was building up an impressive reputation in the theatre. He was already known and respected by the time Stan arrived on the scene in 1890, but he was to climb to even greater things and inevitably the family was destined to live something of a nomadic life, following A. J. around the North of England as his career took him towards the top. Inevitably also, it meant periods of separation. Although Stan was left at Ulverston through his very early years the family remained close. The Jeffersons must have thought that staying at home with his grandparents would give him more stability than the travels from town to town, theatre to theatre. Stan recalled later: "We were seldom together. It was almost always either in boarding school or living with my grandparents in Ulverston, but still, strange as it may seem, we were always a close family."

Before Stan's birth, his parents had been living in the North East, at Bishop Auckland where A. J. was manager of the Old Theatre Royal. Madge came home to her mother for the birth which was a difficult one from which she took some time to recover. Later the Jeffersons moved to South View, Bishop Auckland, where Stan's sister Beatrice Olga was born. Five year old Stan was brought over from Ulverston for the christening of his sister in St Peter's

South View, Bishop Auckland. Beatrice was born in a house in this street, it was the second home of the Jefferson's in the town.

Church, Bishop Auckland, and was re-christened there himself at the same time — January 3, 1895. His first christening had been at home in Argyle Street, Ulverston, because of his illness. Although Beatrice remained with her parents, Stan returned to his grandparents for another two years, spending only brief holidays with his mother, father, brother and sister.

Stan finally left Ulverston when he was about six years old and went to school in Bishop Auckland, but he continued to spend most of his school holidays with Grandma and Granda Metcalfe in Ulverston, and also visited the Shaws who were still at Sawrey. In 1906 the Shaw family moved from the grocery store in Sawrey to Batley in Yorkshire. John Shaw, who came originally from the Batley area, was worried about work prospects for his family and wanted to return to an area where they would be able to get employment. Although the Shaws, particularly Mary, loved life in the Lake District they wrenched themselves away, packing all their

St. Peter's Church, Bishop Auckland where Stan and Beatrice were christened together.

belongings and moving to a house in Lady Ann Road, Batley. John began work in a woollen mill and his daughter Mary, by now an accomplished piano player, gave lessons, sometimes from her home in Lady Ann Road, and sometimes at her pupils' houses. John later went into the rag merchants' business with his brother.

King James the First Grammar School, Bishop Auckland, one of Stan's schools.

It was always the idea that Grandma and Granda Metcalfe would join them as soon as they found a suitable home. Grandma, although still as cheerful as ever, was suffering from arthritis and the Shaws left their third daughter, Nellie, in Ulverston to help the couple. A year later a house became vacant in Batley on the opposite side of the road from the Shaws, and the Metcalfes, their furniture and belongings, were soon settled in a new home. Nellie rejoined her parents.

Stan, by this time, was working in the theatre, but continued to be a regular visitor to his grandparents and the Shaws in Lady Ann Road whenever holidays allowed. Nancy Wardell remembers her mother speaking of his visits. He was often seen walking down the street on stilts to meet her from work, much to her embarrassment and the amusement of other passers-by. Later the Shaw and Metcalfe families moved again and settled together at South View, Soothill, close to their old home. After the death of Stan's mother in

*Lady Ann Road —
Stan's practising
ground for stilt
walking.*

*Mill Lane School,
where Stan met his
younger brother Teddy
from school.*

69

*85 Warwick Road, as
it looks today.*

1908, the family brought Teddy, Stan's younger brother, to live with them here. It is coincidence that their home had the same name as the Jefferson's home years earlier in Bishop Auckland.

Soon after Teddy joined the family, they were on the move again to a larger house, 85 Warwick Road, Batley, a three storey Victorian property where there was room for them all — by this time there were 11 of them to house, Grandma and Granda, John and Nant Shaw, their six children and Teddy. Stan visited as before, and a school friend of Teddy's remembered the comedian fetching his younger brother for tea from his Mill Lane School close by. All the Shaw children, including Mary, were married from Warwick Road, to local people. Mary married Herbert Jennings and moved to 1 Off East Bath Street where their daughter Nancy was born and later moved with her husband Clarence Wardell just round the corner to 24 East Bath Street.

Granda Metcalfe died at Warwick Road in April 1915, aged 78. Grandma died there too within a year. Teddy moved to America to join his brother Stan and with little need of the big old house when they were finally alone, John and Nant Shaw moved to a smaller house in Crackenedge Lane, Dewsbury where they had fine views across the town. In 1960 Mary and Herbert Jennings, moved with their daughter Nancy and her husband Clarence to a new home in Ullswater Road, Dewsbury. Within a few weeks Herbert died and four years later Nancy and Clarence took Mary with them to Ennerdale Crescent, Dewsbury. On one of Mary's birthdays, the Wardell's named the house "Ulverston", after the place she had loved as a child, and they bought a wooden plaque to put up on the house, much to Mary's delight. Sadly Nancy's husband died in 1968 and her mother two years later. Nancy still lives at "Ulverston" where the original plaque has been replaced with one made of Westmorland slate. It was given to Nancy by Bill Cubin, the keen Laurel and Hardy fan from the town of Ulverston.

Nancy at "Ulverston"
behind is the
Westmorland Slate
sign.

Cousins Nellie, Mary and Elsie, growing up.

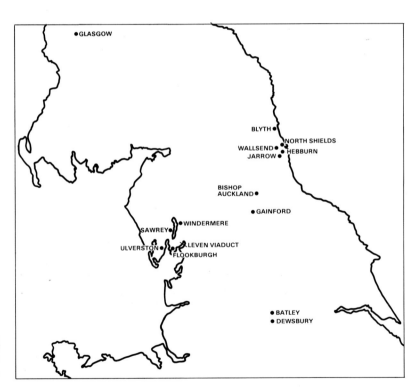

A map charting
Stan's moves and
memories in
northern Britain.

Chapter Eleven
Learning for Laughs

Between the time Stan left his grandparents in Ulverston and 1906, a space of around ten years, he attended several schools at Bishop Auckland, Gainford, and Glasgow. He also talked later in a letter to a fan of attending school in Tynemouth, just after the Boer War, but we have been unable to trace which one. About the time that Stan went to school in Bishop Auckland, his father became manager of the Theatre Royal in North Shields and moved with Madge to 8, Dockwray Square in the town. He was also manager and lessee of the New Theatre Royal, Blyth, the Theatre Royal, Wallsend, and the New Theatre Royal, Hebburn. He was writing plays and managing touring companies which were playing all over the country, and Madge, who had proved herself a talented actress, travelled with him. It was boarding school for Stan, but he quickly settled in and learnt for the first time that he could make people laugh with his clowning around. Stan was at school when his brother Sydney Everitt was born on April 30, 1899 at the family home in Dockwray Square. He was christened at Christ Church, North Shields, but died within a few months.

Stan spent about three years at his Bishop Auckland boarding school and although he was not renowned for his academic brilliance, he was as a laughter maker. It was here that he performed

Stan and the children's nurse.

Dockwray Square, North Shields which has now sadly vanished from the scene. The Jefferson's home has been pulled down. Theirs, was one of the houses in the shade on the left hand side of the picture.

in a make shift way for his first audience outside the family circle. A special admirer was one of Stan's teachers, Mr. Bates, and when he was an internationally acclaimed comic, Stan remembered how Mr. Bates would call him to his study to entertain him and other masters who were relaxing after school. "I must have been awful," he recalled, "but they seemed to get a big kick out of it and I played many return engagements there".

If it was well known at school that Stan was a budding comic, it certainly was not at home. A. J. and Madge were aware that their son was taking a keen interest in the theatre and in A. J.'s great love of drama. During one of his holidays from school Stan pleaded with his father to let him convert the attic of their home in North Shields to a small theatre where he and his friends could put on their own mini productions.

In a biography on his son, written when A. J. was 75, he recalled: "I agreed, calling upon my local theatre staff to carry out the work (in which they evinced great pleasure) producing very creditable results, stage, proscenium, wings etc and footlights (the

A. J.'s theatre in North Shields — the Theatre Royal.

Prudhoe Street, North Shields. 6881

latter being oil lamps with reflectors, safer than gas we thought). With seating capacity for about 20 to 30 people, in brief a replica of the average small theatre at that period."

It allowed nine year old Stan to form the Stanley Jefferson Amateur Dramatic Society in which he took on most of the roles from managing director to leading actor in plays which he also wrote. He enlisted the help of young friends to act in his dramas, some apparently not always as willing as he would have liked! We know, for instance, that cousin Mary, who was always roped in during her visits to North Shields, would have preferred to play the piano.

A. J. recalled how his son would charge admission fees for his productions, and if not actual cash, members of the audience would be admitted for all kinds of props that might come in handy for later plays. In fact Stan collected quite an assortment of clothes, rugs, curtains and other items. As for the audience itself, Stan would not play to an empty theatre and when the house did not look like filling up he would apparently race round the rest of the rooms and sometimes up and down the street dragging people in to watch his masterpieces.

The final performance in the attic was to be talked about for months and years to come. It was a particularly bloodthirsty piece, according to A. J., in which Stan and the 'villain' (the butcher's son, Harold) acted out a 'fight to the death' when Stan had finally tracked down the murderer (poor Harold). As they grappled on the boards Harold kicked over one of the paraffin oil lamps and the curtains caught fire. A. J. arrived to find the audience fleeing down the stairs crying 'Fire'. Harold and Stan both sustained minor burns, (apparently Harold singed and lost his eyebrows) but more tragically for Stan, he lost the theatre. It severely put back his friendship with little Harold! A few days later, while Stan was still getting over the grief of the final scene in his play, he received a letter from Harold, blaming him for the loss of the eyebrows and demanding back his subscription to the theatre — two white mice. Stan was livid and after consulting A. J. sent his former friend a stinging letter reminding him that he too had been injured and had lost his theatre. "Dad is having it all done away with for good and all my pocket money since it started," he complained. Stan refused to return the white mice but generously offered to give Harold one of the babies "if they ever get married," and he finished his letter "If you want to be friends I do, if you don't, I don't, Stanley."

Meanwhile back at Bishop Auckland Stan was having other problems. He may have impressed Mr Bates, but other teachers were not quite so happy with his achievements. Stan later remembered the German master's exasperation with him during lessons. "He had the habit of carrying a pencil crosswise in his mouth and when I couldn't answer his questions in class, he used to go into a frenzy," he said "He'd chew that pencil up into pieces and spit them out of his mouth in disgust." Stan made the mistake of imitating the teacher during one of his appearances before Mr. Bates, and other members of staff including the German master. Although most of his audience seemed to appreciate the act, the German master was apparently not amused. Stan characteristically

The front view of the Gainford Academy.

was unmoved. He said later: "What I did, I did trying to make the masters enjoy themselves. Anything for a laugh!"

A. J. was not amused either at his son's slow academic progress and eventually he took him away from Bishop Auckland.

He put him into a school in Gainford where he hoped for better results! It must have been a great blow to young Stan, but he was well aware of his shortcomings. He wrote: "I don't think playing to Bates and the other masters helped my education any as I was given a lot of privileges and a lot of my backwardness in class was overlooked which many times since I've regretted . . . those were happy days at Bishop Auckland."

Stan arrived at Gainford, aged about 10 years old. It must have been quite an upheaval for the little boy, but his perseverance was rewarded a year later when his father took over The Metropole

Stan taken in North Shields

*Nurse, Beatrice and
baby Teddy.*

Theatre in Glasgow and moved the entire family to his new base. The Post Office Directories for Glasgow show that from 1905 to 1906 the family lived at Buchanan Drive, Rutherglen. There is no further mention of a home address, possibly because they were living in rented accommodation.

Just before the move, there was another addition to the Jefferson household. Edward Everitt was born on April 1, 1901 in Dockwray Square and christened there at Christ Church.

In the autumn of 1901 Stan set off for his first day at another school, Queen's Park, Glasgow. Stan probably already had a good idea of what he wanted to do when he left school and teachers found it very hard to make him concentrate in class. A. J. had not given up however and Stan was transferred to yet another establishment, Rutherglen School, Glasgow, where he finished his education in 1906 at the age of 16. At the end of Stan's last term A. J. set him to work on various jobs at the Metropole Theatre. He was not too worried about Stan's indifferent career at school and thought that he would eventually take over as assistant manager at the Glasgow theatre. But he had not reckoned with Stan's burning ambition to act. What A. J. did not know was that Stan was spending many hours in front of his bedroom mirror practising with borrowed stage make-up and costume. His mother was well aware of his ambitions and although she was by this time virtually bedridden she gave him terrific encouragement. Mother and son spent many happy hours talking about the theatre, the players of the day and Madge's own achievements on the stage.

Grandma Metcalfe was not enamoured with Stan's ideas. When he told her of his intentions on visits to Batley she always reminded him of the heartaches, the nomadic life and uncertainty of the theatre. She must have been thinking of her daughter's life and of Stan's own young life, being moved from home to home, catching what time he could with his busy parents. But the theatre was already flowing deeply in the Jefferson blood. Stan's brother Gordon was showing some talent, although times were hard for him and he had to cable home from Belgium more than once when

*Grandma Metcalfe in
later years.*

*A portrait picture of
Mrs. John Shaw —
Auntie Nant.*

*John Shaw — Stan's
Uncle.*

Stan, a photo sent home in March 1911.

*Stan's sister, Beatrice
Olga.*

— *Pictures from her
theatre days* —

Cousin George.

*Cousin Mary, Nancy
Wardell's mother.*

Madge, posing in North Shields.

money was short. Sister Beatrice, too, seemed determined to follow her parents into the theatre, although she was to spend some time in a convent in Belgium first.

Stan made his debut as a comic at the Pickard Theatre, Glasgow, in 1906, apparently without his father's knowledge. Legend has it that by pure chance A. J. visited A. E. Pickard's Glasgow Museum that night and witnessed his son's first public performance — a mixture of songs, jokes and dancing. It is said that Stan was horrified when he caught sight of his father at the end of his act, but although it had been quite a shock to Stan on stage, A. J. was quite impressed with the act, if not quite so enamoured with the material. It was probably this episode that convinced A. J. he was fighting a losing battle trying to keep his son on 'front of house' work and the following year he found him a place with Levy and Cardwell's Juvenile Pantomimes, a group of youngsters aged between six and 18 all vying for stardom. Stan stayed with them for two years as stage manager.

Chapter Twelve

A. J. — Success and Failure

A. J. had already trudged the road of struggles and poverty which Stan was yet to know, and by the time his son left school he was a comparatively wealthy man with a string of successes behind him. It was a far cry from the days of the Gaff, the makeshift wooden theatre in Ulverston where many of his melodramas had their first showing. In 1889, five years after his marriage to Madge Metcalfe, A. J. took over the Old Theatre Royal in Bishop Auckland with a partner called Thorn. They ran the theatre together for two years until Mr Thorn bought himself out. A. J. carried on alone for two seasons and then he and Madge pulled the theatre apart and redesigned it. They changed the name to the Eden Theatre, after getting permission from a famous local family to use their name. Madge and A. J. set up their first home together in Tenter Street, Bishop Auckland and later moved to South View in the same town. It was during this period that A. J. took over the management of a group of American illusionists called The Sheens. They appeared at The Eden, and A. J. arranged tours for them in other English theatres.

He was also writing plays and his 'World's Verdict' was shown around this time. It had its premier at Shildon in 1893. Steadily his theatrical empire grew and he used Bishop Auckland as the base for his touring companies which travelled throughout Britain and on the continent. In 1893 he reopened the Theatre Royal at Consett and a year later took over and opened the Old Theatre Royal at Blyth. In a letter to a fan, Mrs. Short in England in May 1957, Stan wrote: "I remember the old theatre (at Blyth) that was on the same site when my Dad was running it, it was a very run down affair — benches instead of chairs, sawdust on the floors, cement stairs to the gallery. Gas was the only lighting, it used to play old time melodramas and was nick-named The Blood Tub. Anyway it used to do wonderful business and the place was always packed. My Dad felt very grateful to the people of Blyth for their generous support and thought it would be a nice gesture to show his appreciation by building a nice new modern theatre for their pleasure and entertainment, he thought they deserved it in turn for their wonderful patronage in the past."

Records show that a new theatre was built on the site of the Old Theatre Royal at a cost of some £14,000. Stan told Mrs Short: "Well he invested a great deal of money and the New Theatre Royal was erected, the most modern theatre of its time, electric lighting, the floors were carpeted, tip up red velvet chairs etc, Lifts instead of stairs to the Balcony and Gallery, even had a nursery with nurses in attendance to take care of the children so the parents and others in the audience wouldn't be disturbed during the performance. The orchestra were in evening dress the Stage crew in white uniforms, also the program and chocolate boys dressed as page boys with white gloves, not a thing was spared."

But it was a disaster — Stan told Mrs. Short: "Believe it or not it turned out a fiasco. The place was too elegant and the people wouldn't come in, they liked the sawdust and wooden benches much better, they felt out of place in the beautiful surroundings, I imagine the feeling was they would have to be dressed up instead of coming in their weekday clothes, so the only time they did come was Saturday night wearing their Sunday suit! It broke my Dad financially so he gave it up along with his other theatres in North Shields, Jarrow, Hebburn and Wallsend and we moved to Glasgow where he took control of the old Metropole Theatre, wasn't that awful? Yes I have a memory of Blyth I shall never forget?

But the memories of the Jefferson family's time in the theatres of Northern England were certainly not all bad and the move to Scotland was still some seven years off, when A. J. first took over the Blyth theatre. It was 1895 when he took over the Theatre Royal at North Shields, along with those at Wallsend, Hebburn and Jarrow. At the same time he was proprietor of the Borough of Tynemouth Circus and Novelty Hippodrome and managing director of the North British Animated Picture Company.

The people of Bishop Auckland had come to regard their local celebrities as "almost townspeople" and were distressed when Madge and A. J. abandoned the town in 1895 and moved to North Shields where they settled in Dockwray Square, closer to A. J.'s growing new empire in the North East. He left a manager to look after the Eden Theatre. By the time he arrived in North Shields, A. J. had three of his plays on tour 'Orphan Heiress', 'Royal Divorce' and 'Bootblack'.

With his talent for producing good theatre he had taken the family from its poverty stricken days of the 1880's, scurrying about the country to make a living, to a new era when Stan was able to attend boarding school and they could afford a comfortable home and a nurse for the children. Stan once recalled in a letter to a British fan: "I remember when my Dad built the place (Blyth) . . . I was going to school at the time in Tynemouth, it was just after the Boer War, he also ran the Theatre Royal in North Shields, and the Boro, also had theatres in Jarrow, Hebburn and Wallsend, what memories."

Shortly before his death Stan wrote of the Old Theatre Royal at Blyth: "It was indeed in those days a beautiful theatre, complete in every detail, a credit to any community. I hope it will be considered and converted into a civic auditorium and will be spared destruction — I feel the building has historic value as a landmark and should be preserved. The town and district need such a place to hold their local meetings and important affairs, besides establishing talent and local culture in the future."

GRAND THEATRE
AND OPERA HOUSE,
COWCADDENS, GLASGOW.

Lessee and Manager ... (To whom all communications be addressed.) ... Mr ERNEST STEVENS.
Secretary ... ... Mr JOHN BRANGWIN.

MONDAY, 26th APRIL, and during the Week,

ARTHUR JEFFERSON'S COMPANY,

In the Successful Domestic and Comedy Drama—THE

ORPHAN HEIRESS

By ARTHUR JEFFERSON, Author of "———'s Verdict," and "The Bootblack."

Lord Warwick Ainsley............(a We—maker)	...........Mr William Vernon
Douglas Kingston...............(his Co— Clerk)...........	...Mr Charles Boult
Lawrence Gordon........(a Bank Clerk— with Mabel)...Mr Villiers Stanley
Ginger ? ? ? ? ? ?....................................Mr J. E. Coyle
Rev. Edward Ayrton............(Vicar — lands)........Mr Charles Girdlestone
Martin Craven.................(a M——ter)...............Mr Harry Stainton
Sandien Loski (Loski's Continental C— Hippodrome) Mr Taliesyn G. Davies
Jenkins...................................(a—............Mr James O'Conner
Williams...................................(a—...............Mr W. Bowers
Alfred Murray...................(Inspec— Police)............Mr George M'Closky
Tate.............................(a D—e).......................Mr Aylesbury
P.C. Smith...Mr E. Charles Nunn
Pierre....................... ...(the A—ler)...............Mr Robert Burton
Verne.......................(Captain —armes)................Mr Alfred Webb
Mabel Ainsley (the Heiress, daughter— and Lady Ainsley) Miss Marie Robson
Edith Mowbray....{ Housekeeper to L—wick Ainsley, and} Miss Ella Vane
{ devoted friend— Wife and Child }
Lady Laura Ainsley...{ Wife of Lord W— Ainsley, Mother} Miss Loyale Frere
{ of Ma— Heiress }
Olive Kingston...(Sister of Douglas K—well matched)...Miss Mara Collings
Betsy Buggles..............(Ginger's happ—d sorrow)........Miss Lillie Winter
Janette... ....(A French — Maid)... Miss Gertrude Grenville

Servants, Grooms, Wai— endarmes, Police, &c.

Act 1 ... ... Reception — at Earlsmere Court, Surrey
Lord Warwick A—y's Residence.
Between Acts 1 and — val of 13 minutes.

Act 2—Scene 1 ... ... Beech Lane, Woodlands
Scene 2 ... ... —nge and Grounds, Woodlands
Between Acts 2 and — val of 10 minutes.

Act 3—Scene 1 ... ... Library at Earlsmere Court
Scene 2 ... ... Street in London
Scene 3 ... ... —or of Ainsley's Bank, London
Scene 4 ... ... —Strong Room in Ainsley's Bank
Between Acts 3 and — val of 10 minutes.

Act 4—Scene 1 ... ... Victor's Hotel, Paris
Scene 2 ... ... Street in Paris
Scene 3 ... ... Dressing Tent, the Circus

In this Scene, Specialities will be intro— —*quarious Members of the Company.*

Scene 4, Ante-tent of —a— —n Continental Circus and Hippodrome
INTR—

The Cage of Deat— Who are you?

NOTE.—The Curtain will descend on — Situation for a few seconds only.

Kingston and Loski Outwitted— —he Heiress asserts her Claim.

Business Manager...............} For "Orphan —" Company { ...Mr E. Parker-Royston
Stage Manager..................}   {.......Mr J. E. Coyle

*Bill for the Orphan
Heiress, performed by
Arthur Jefferson's
Company at the Grand
Theatre.*

96

Stan's fans in England took a keen interest in all the theatres that he and his father had been connected with in the early years of the century. When he got news of plans for the theatre in North Shields where his father had been such a popular show business figure, he said, on Jan 6, 1958: "I understand great changes are being made in North Shields. Dockwray Square where I used to live is all being torn away to make way for new flats. The old Boro theatre that my Dad originally built has closed for good and they are going to have a brand new wooden dolly, they are sure fixing up the old town. All the old landmarks are gradually disappearing — everybody will soon have to wear their Sunday clothes every day."

It was 1901 when A. J. moved the family to Glasgow and his arrival at the Metropole was greeted with great excitement by the theatre-going public and those who wrote about it in the early 1900's. In 1901 Captain Slingsley wrote in the Yorkshire Post: "A truly wonderful man is this Mr Jefferson. He has just opened another theatre in Glasgow in Stockwell Street. I may inform my Bradfordians who are visiting the exhibition, his fifth so far, he is only forty years of age and the author of 'The Orphan Heiress' and many other dramas."

The Victualling Trades' Review was equally ecstatic about the arrival of the Jeffersons. Pictures of Madge and A. J. appeared in the review and readers were told: "Mr Jefferson is ably assisted by his good lady under whose supervision the decorations have been so handsomely carried out in the Metropole this summer. We have much pleasure in including their photos in our 'Portrait Gallery' and wishing to the pair a long career of happiness and prosperity."

In the same feature the Review announced: "It would be difficult to find a better example of theatrical enterprise than is apparent at the Metropole Theatre since it came under the sway of Mr Arthur Jefferson, the present lessee. Altered, re-arranged and brought thoroughly up to date in every particular, the Metropole is one of the most comfortable and capacious temples of the drama in Scotland. Quite recently the whole interior has been again overhauled and the auditorium fresh from the hands of the

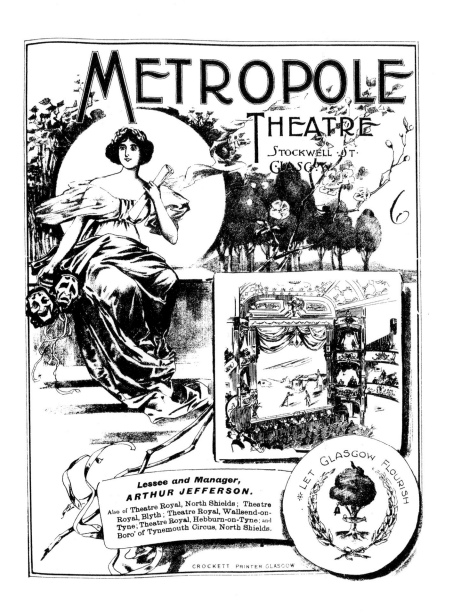

decorators Messrs J. and R. Anderson of Bath Street, Glasgow, improved in a manner beyond recognition, the style of treatment and harmony of colours being in every instance both appropriate and artistic."

It was of course, the work of Mrs. Jefferson which brought such praise. And of A. J.? . . . "Since the advent of Mr. Jefferson some weeks ago, it became quite evident that his intention was to maintain for the Metropole the very highest standard of excellence and in this he has eminently succeeded by securing the leading London and Provincial Touring companies in one continuous line of succession. This, added to his energetic and skilful management and the strong influence of his own personality and experience in the professional world, have crowned the undertaking with unparalleled success and for this alone we feel constrained to add, the whole theatre-going population of the west of Scotland owe him a debt of gratitude. Of Mr. Jefferson it may truly be said "He came, saw and conquered," but like Peter the Great his unimpaired energies are still seeking for further outlet and other worlds to conquer."

A. J. had already made a name for himself as an author and playwright and when the Review published its glowing article on him he had two plays on tour, 'The Orphan Heiress,' and, 'London by Day and Night'. On July 14, 1901 the theatre critic at the Rochdale Times published his piece on 'London by Day and Night' after seeing the play performed by A. J.'s No. 1 company:

"There are many features which do not fail to give the utmost satisfaction and pleasure," he wrote. "Humour and pathos are admirably blended and whilst the latter is not too painfully evident the former is not overdone. At the same time the plot is arranged in such a way as to allow for the enactments of numerous thrilling incidents and though it is complicated as melodramatic plots usually are its leading movements can be easily followed by the unsophisticated playgoer"

A month later the Glasgow Programme advertised yet another of A. J.'s plays, 'A Royal Divorce,' being performed at the

The cigarette case presented to A.J. when he left the Eden Theatre.

Metropole. "The Metropole under Mr. Arthur Jefferson has never had such a run of business," it proclaimed, "since it was a theatre, everything is so well managed and so carefully supervised that the large middle class for whom this theatre caters specially, are answering the call by attending in very large numbers. This week we are having a return visit of that marvellous attraction entitled 'A Royal Divorce.' "

A. J. made Glasgow his base for the next 23 years and it was here that his wife Madge died on September 1st 1908 after a long illness. She was buried at Cathcart Cemetery, Glasgow. Her obituary in a Glasgow newspaper said: "Widespread regret not only amidst the ranks of the theatrical profession, but also those of social circles in the various towns with which her name has been associated, was manifested when it became known that Mrs. Arthur Jefferson, professionally known as Madge Metcalfe, had passed away in Glasgow. The numerous telegrams and letters of condolence from all parts of the country bear eloquent testimony to the chain of friendships she had forged in her theatrical career. Prior to her marriage she was not in any way theatrically connected and it speaks columns for her abilities and energy to find that she was soon afterwards playing the leading 'heavy' roles in her husband's plays. Her most important part was Olga Snake in The Bootblack in which she excelled, and beautifully gowned made a most imposing appearance. The press in every town visited and accorded her its unstinted and certainly well deserved praise. In addition to acting she proved an invaluable aid to her husband in the decoration schemes for his various theatres and play staging and he attributes much of his early success to her artistic taste in that affection as well as her business tact."

Madge's death must have been a bitter blow to Arthur Jefferson, but he continued in his theatrical career and took a keen interest in the developing talent of his son, who was to leave for fame in America two years later, travelling by cattle boat with the Fred Karno company. It was tough for Stan as well, who was just embarking on his career and he later recalled the agony of going on stage to perform his act just after hearing the news of his mother's death.

In 1922 A. J. was called back to the Eden Theatre, Bishop Auckland, which was struggling under its previous manager and had been closed down in 1921 by the police on safety grounds. It was then bought by two Bishop Auckland businessmen — a solicitor and a paper merchant — who altered the old A. J. style theatre dramatically. They opened it a year later with a manager from Stockton. He lasted three months. A. J.'s reputation was still widespread and the two businessmen managed to persuade him to leave his Scottish home and take over the Eden again.

He was in his 60's when he arrived back in Bishop Auckland and the theatre already had strong competition from cinemas. A. J. tried everything, bringing former stars of the theatre to the town, but they also were past their best. Finally beaten, A. J. left the Eden in September 1925 and moved to London. The staff of the theatre presented him with a silver cigarette case which is now on display amongst other memorabilia in the Laurel and Hardy Museum at Ulverston.

In 1958 Mrs. Short, writing from the North of England, jogged Stan's memory of the Eden days with a newspaper clipping about a pantomime which had opened there. He told her: "Funny thing, the article mentions the Pantomime opened in Bishop Auckland (Durham) that was another of my Dad's theatres which he leased for several years — the Eden theatre and I used to board at the King James Grammar School in B.A. which is still in existence. I think I have the honour of been the worst scholar that ever attended there"! His grammar confirmed what he had written of his school days in Bishop Auckland!

After his move to London A. J. continued to act as a booking agent for the Eden Theatre, retaining his link with the town. But he broke even this link in 1927, and his great career finally ended. He died in 1949 and is buried in Grantham Lincolnshire, close to where his daughter Beatrice and her husband ran a pub in Bottesford.

Chapter Thirteen
The Bottom Rung

It seemed that as Stan's career began to take off, his father's fortunes failed. But his encouragement for Stan and his ventures never faltered. In a radio interview in America shortly after the death of Oliver Hardy in the summer of 1957, Stan spoke about his partnership with Babe and his earlier struggle in the theatre. He said his father had never objected to any of his career moves or tried to dissuade him because of his own experiences. "He wouldn't for the world have interfered," he said, "with anything I wanted to do. He helped me as much as he possibly could, things had broken kind of bad for Dad, he lost the theatres and things were not so hot for him, so of course I was getting on now, I was about 21 or 22 years old."

It was in A. J.'s theatres around the North of England that Stan had his first taste of theatrical life. "I dabbled around, some nights in the box office, some nights checking programmes and selling chocolates — general utility, message boy etc," he said. It was now that Stan was secretly trying his hand at vaudeville. "I went to see music hall shows. I had quite a lisp at the time, my voice was broken and I wasn't fitting for anything but a comic," he recalled. "So I decided that was my forte. Anyway my Dad found out that was my desire and immediately got me a job with Levy and Cardwell." Stan started at the bottom in the juvenile pantomime troupe. He later remembered how he traipsed around during the day giving out bills and in the evening he would help with the baggage as the company arrived to put on shows at theatres in the North. Eventually he had a part in the shows as well. The star was to be a life long friend, Wee Georgie Wood.

'The Sleeping Beauty' was running during Stan's first season. Wee Georgie's toys came to life when he fell asleep and in particular Stan remembered two golliwogs in the show: "I wore blue pants, red or blue coat, a big black face and white eyes and mouth, like a rag doll," he said. Stan remained with the company for two seasons, the second of which saw a pantomime called 'The House that Jack Built.' He ended up as assistant stage manager but still he wanted to go further. "I got a good taste of the business and I decided I wanted to go out on my own as a boy comedian," he said "so I made ventures into variety but I wasn't too successful" . . . It was back to Dad.

Around this time in 1908 A. J. was running a successful vaudeville piece he called 'Home from the Honeymoon' which was playing in the big Moss Empire houses. Stan continued his training with the show as assistant manager. After several weeks A. J. lost one of the comedians in the sketch and put Stan in his place for the remainder of the season. "After that I continued to try out my luck as a boy comedian. I didn't get too far, I was just at an awkward age," Stan remembered.

Eventually with the help of his father, Stan joined the Fred Karno troupe. Charlie Chaplin was the main comedian when Stan joined and Stan became his understudy. But fortune did not come straight away. On that first trip with Fred Karno to America, Stan was earning just 20 dollars a week and he said later: "When you're travelling, we had to pay our own sleepers, hotels, food and what have you, even though everything was very cheap at that time, still 20 dollars wasn't enough to travel on and take care of yourself, so it ended up with three or four of us sharing a room."

Stan and a few of his fellow players asked for more money, but they were refused a rise and Stan left the troupe in Colorado Springs

*Stan — in costume,
the days of carrotty
hair, a lisp, and
breaking voice.*

Postcard sent home by Stan while he was travelling.

and returned to England, no better off than when he had first arrived. He soon put an act together with another comedian, Arthur Dando, and they called themselves the Barto Brothers, putting on a pantomime which brought them success in England. "There was a little talk in it, but it was mostly pantomime," Stan recalled. "We did a kind of Roman skit and we called it the 'Rum Uns from Rome.' We put on grotesque make-up and had a chariot with no bottom so you saw feet walking." The act was short lived. Dando got a better offer and Stan was back on his own. Quickly he found another partner, Ted Leo, who later became a dance orchestra leader. "We didn't get very far with it," mused Stan. Leo had an old partner, Bob Read, who had just got a contract to put his Eight Comics on the stage all over the continent. He wanted Ted Leo to go with them. It must have been a break for Ted, but he felt guilty about leaving Stan in the lurch and eventually both of them joined the company and set off to play in Holland, Belgium and France.

The whole thing was a flop. It seemed the troupe hardly got a chance to perform at all as it rained nearly every day. Eventually they arrived, downhearted, in Belgium to play in a night club. But of course the Eight Comics were not what the Belgium night club had in mind for the evening's entertainment. "We were cancelled after the first show," said Stan "so we had to get back to England the best way we could."

It must have been the kind of experience that A. J. had dreaded. It was the sort of nightmare that had probably made him hope that Stan would make his career front of house. Stan's brother Gordon was now making his own way in the theatre and at the time of Stan's disaster on the continent was managing the Princess Theatre in London "I was down and out practically," Stan recalled more than 50 years later, "I didn't have a dime. He got me a room in his flat and a job in a show called 'Ben MacRee."

Stan got another job typing and was just getting back on his feet when he bumped into Alf Reeves, the American manager for the Fred Karno outfit. Mr. Reeves offered him the rise he had asked for before returning to England and his place back in the Karno troupe.

Postcard sent home to Stan's grandparents.

Stan packed his bags and rejoined Charlie Chaplin and the others. But the heartaches were not yet over. The troupe was just about to set off on tour with a show called 'Jimmy the Fearless' when Chaplin suddenly announced he did not want to do it. Karno picked Stan out of the troupe and gave him Chaplin's part.

"We opened at the Hippodrome in West Ealing, London," said Stan. "The show was quite a success. I was congratulated by everybody. Well Chaplin sat in front for two or three shows and decided he liked the part so I was thrown back in the chorus." Poor Stan! It was back to the drawing board and he was never destined to make principal comedian with Fred Karno. But Chaplin was under contract and the part was his for the asking.

Throughout this period Stan kept in close contact with his relations in the North of England and his visits to Batley were frequent. When he could not get there in person he would keep in touch, sending postcards to his grandparents and the others from wherever he happened to be. When he left for the States with Fred Karno a couple of months after the 'Jimmy the Fearless' disappointment, it was the last time he looked upon England as his real home. Although he continued to write to friends and relations regularly, kept up with all the news, and made tours here, later with Ollie, home was now America.

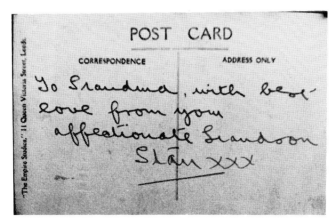

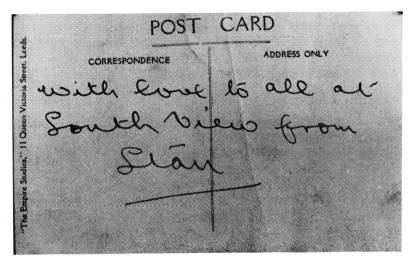

Brief message on the back of Stan's postcard as he kept in touch with his family in the North of England.

Chapter Fourteen
Laurel is Born

Shortly after Stan's return to the States with the Fred Karno outfit, Charlie Chaplin was lured away to Hollywood with Mack Sennet. The company was about to open in Philadelphia with Chaplin top of the bill. Once again Stan was given his chance to step into the limelight. "But the outfit running the shows refused to take me," recalled Stan, "they wanted another comedian, a principal comedian from England, they wanted a London star name, so I lost out again." Karno cabled London and the 'principal comedian' arrived. But in Stan's words: "The show was a terrible flop, he just didn't fit, so the show folded in three weeks."

Most of the troupe returned to England, but Stan had learnt his lesson. He remained in the States and joined forces with two other survivors from the troupe, Edgar Hurley and his wife. The new partners called themselves The Three Comiques and put together an act called 'The Nutty Burglars.' "We didn't play anything of any note we were happy to make a living and enjoy ourselves," said Stan later. They succeeded however in making an impression on one of their fellow show business colleagues in Cleveland. He told them he thought they would do well on the stage in New York. But when they heard no more they moved on to Pittsburgh. It was there they received a telegram asking them to perform their show in New

Ollie and Stan, the laughter kings — a picture sent to Nancy Wardell.

Jersey. They changed their names, opened in New Jersey and were an instant hit. Now it was suggested that they change their names to The Keystone Trio with Stan making up as Charlie Chaplin, Edgar Hurley doing Chester Conklin and his wife being the 'Mable Normand' character. This was the start of an era of Charlie Chaplin impersonators. Stan claimed he was the first and others followed him. The formula was certainly a success, but it was not to last.

Edgar Hurley and Stan fell out over the Charlie Chaplin part. "My partner got jealous," Stan said later. "He wanted to do Charlie Chaplin. It was a disastrous thing, he did it for one performance. Finally it got to words and we decided to split." Edgar Hurley took another partner, Teddy Banks, and Stan found two more partners and carried on with the same sort of material. By this time it seemed everybody had got on the Charlie Chaplin/Chester Conklin bandwagon and Stan decided it was time for a change. He formed the Stan Jefferson Trio with a husband and wife team, Baldwin and Alice Cooke. It was the summer of 1916. The three of them put an act together called the 'Crazy Cracksman.' They took to the road and set about earning a living. "It was four or five shows a day, seven nights a week," said Stan. "It was very hard work . . . when you worked."

The Stan Jefferson Trio lasted until 1918 when he split with Alice and Baldwin and formed a duo he called Stan and Mae Laurel. Finally he had changed his name, but he always said he had no idea why, except that he had never been happy with Jefferson. "I changed the name on account of billing," he said, "Jefferson was quite a long name so it always appeared smaller on the billing on that account. So I though if I had a shorter name the letters would be bigger, it turned out OK, I've no idea why it was Laurel, no idea." It was Mae, who took the credit for finding the name. She said she had been looking at a history book in a theatre dressing room and saw an etching of Scipio Africanus Major. He had what she thought was a laurel on his head, which turned out to be a wreath of bay leaves, and suggested the name Stan Laurel.

However it happened, the name stuck and Stan and Mae Laurel continued their act — Mae singing and dancing, Stan doing his

Stan's Beverley Hills, a picture sent home.

burglar sketch still with the obligatory red nose. They were playing the Hippodrome, Los Angeles, when Hal Roach's director Alf Goulding spotted Stan and thought he had possibilities in pictures. Roach was looking for someone to finish a series of films when Toto the clown ducked out of a contract. "I went in and completed the five pictures, so it was my introduction to movies," remembered Stan. By now he was tired of the endless nights in theatre and anxious to settle down to a steadier life "and live like a human." He wanted to do more pictures and worked for Larry Semen and Bronco Billy as well as going back on the road between films. It was 1927 when Stan and Oliver Hardy made their first official film together, 'Putting Pants on Philip.' It was the start of the famous partnership that was to bring laughter to millions.

Chapter Fifteen
Letters to a Fan

Recently a series of letters from Stan to one of his fans has come to light in Newcastle Central Library. He always prided himself on answering all his fan mail personally throughout his career, claiming that no letter went unanswered or gift not acknowledged. These letters are proof of that. They show that newspaper cuttings were pored over and comments on them passed back across the ocean to Mr. and Mrs. Short in the North of England.

The letters span a 12 year period of correspondence between the Shorts and Stan. They begin in April 1952, while Stan and Ollie were still playing together and end shortly before Stan's death. The last letter is dated September 1964. Stan died five months later after suffering a heart attack and is buried in Forest Lawn Cemetery. The plaque on his grave reads "STAN LAUREL. A Master of Comedy, His genius in the art of humour brought gladness to the world he loved."

Although not strictly written in the period of Laurel Before Hardy, we have reproduced them on the next few pages, because they contain snippets of Stan's life in the English Theatre, of his father's show business life and comments about his schools. All the letters were presented to Newcastle Central Library by Mrs. Short and are

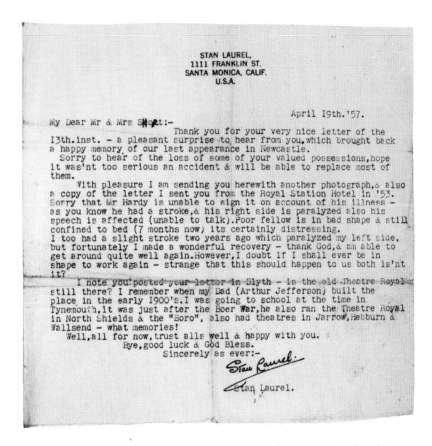

STAN LAUREL,
1111 FRANKLIN ST.
SANTA MONICA, CALIF.
U.S.A.

April 19th.'57.

My Dear Mr & Mrs Short:-
Thank you for your very nice letter of the
13th.inst. - a pleasant surprise to hear from you,which brought back
a happy memory of our last appearance in Newcastle.
Sorry to hear of the loss of some of your valued possessions,hope
it was'nt too serious an accident & will be able to replace most of
them.
With pleasure I am sending you herewith another photograph,& also
a copy of the letter I sent you from the Royal Station Hotel in '53.
Sorry that Mr Hardy is unable to sign it on account of his illness -
as you know he had a stroke,& his right side is paralyzed also his
speech is affected (unable to talk).Poor fellow is in bad shape & still
confined to bed (7 months now) its certainly distressing.
I too had a slight stroke two years ago which paralyzed my left side,
but fortunately I made a wonderful recovery — thank God,& am able to
get around quite well again.However,I doubt if I shall ever be in
shape to work again — strange that this should happen to us both is'nt
it?
I note you posted your letter in Blyth - is the old Theatre Royal
still there? I remember when my Dad (Arthur Jefferson) built the
place in the early 1900's.I was going to school at the time in
Tynemouth,it was just after the Boer War,he also ran the Theatre Royal
in North Shields & the "Boro", also had theatres in Jarrow,Hebburn &
Wallsend — what memories!
Well,all for now,trust alls well & happy with you.
Bye,good luck & God Bless.
Sincerely as ever:-

Stan Laurel.

available for anyone to read. After the death in August 1957 of Stan's
partner Ollie, who had suffered a severe stroke in September 1956, he
did not perform again and he had more time to answer letters from
his fans. In fact it became one of his greatest pleasures to receive fan
mail and sit and answer it all. As a result his letters to the Shorts were
more frequent after 1957 in spite of the fact that he himself collapsed
with a stroke in 1955, leaving him stiff down his left side. It gave him
a great deal of pleasure to hear the news of home and of the theatre
and in those last years memories came flooding back to him and he
shared them with his friends.

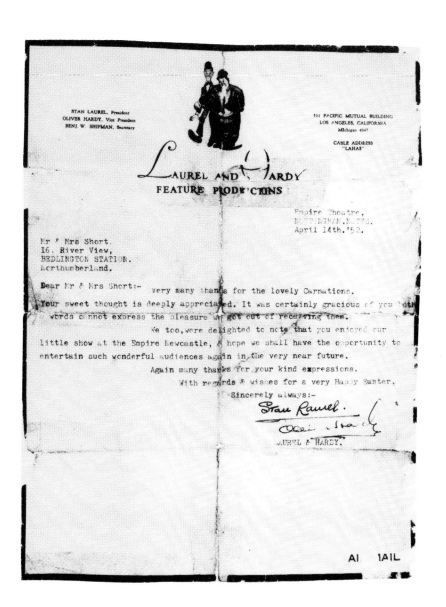

STAN LAUREL, President
OLIVER HARDY, Vice President
BENJ. W. SHIPMAN, Secretary

311 PACIFIC MUTUAL BUILDING
LOS ANGELES, CALIFORNIA
MIchigan 4047

CABLE ADDRESS
"LAHAS"

LAUREL AND HARDY
FEATURE PRODUCTIONS

Empire Theatre,
NOTTINGHAM,NOTTS.
April 14th.'52.

Mr & Mrs Short,
16. River View,
BEDLINGTON STATION.
Northumberland.

Dear Mr & Mrs Short:- very many thanks for the lovely Carnations.
Your sweet thought is deeply appreciated. It was certainly gracious of you both
words cannot express the pleasure we got out of receiving them.

We too, were delighted to note that you enjoyed our
little show at the Empire Newcastle, & hope we shall have the opportunity to
entertain such wonderful audiences again in the very near future.

Again many thanks for your kind expressions.

With regards & wishes for a very Happy Easter,

Sincerely always:-

Stan Laurel.

Oliver Hardy

LAUREL & HARDY.

AIR MAIL

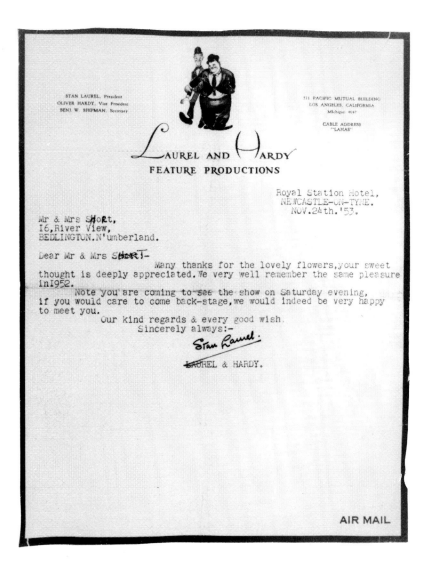

STAN LAUREL, President
OLIVER HARDY, Vice President
BENJ. W. SHIPMAN, Secretary

111 PACIFIC MUTUAL BUILDING
LOS ANGELES, CALIFORNIA
Michigan 4047

CABLE ADDRESS
"LAHAR"

*L*AUREL AND *H*ARDY
FEATURE PRODUCTIONS

Royal Station Hotel,
NEWCASTLE-ON-TYNE.
NOV.24th.'53.

Mr & Mrs SHort,
I6,River View,
BEDLINGTON.N'umberland.

Dear Mr & Mrs SHORT-
          Many thanks for the lovely flowers,your sweet
thought is deeply appreciated.We very well remember the same pleasure
in I952.
          Note you are coming to see the show on Saturday evening,
if you would care to come back-stage,we would indeed be very happy
to meet you.
          Our kind regards & every good wish.
          Sincerely always:-

                    Stan Laurel:

          LAUREL & HARDY.

AIR MAIL

3.

hope I did'nt bore you with the story of the Blyth incident,
but I thought it would be interesting to you.
My kind regards to Mr Short & yourself,trust all is well &
happy.
     Bye now, good luck & God Bless.
        Sincerely always:-
           Stan Laurel.
        Stan Laurel.

May 14th,'57.

Dear Mrs Short:-

Many thanks for your very kind letter of the 6th.inst.Your thoughts & gracious expressions are deeply appreciated.

Pleased to note the picture arrived safely & has given you so much pleasure.It was certainly interesting to know the old Theatre Royal was still in operation - must be going on 60 years old now,I imagine it looks pretty ancient by now I remember the old theatre that was on the same site which my Dad was running,it was a very run down affair - benches instead of chairs,sawdust on the floors,cement stairs to the gallery,gas was the only lighting it had,it used to play old time melodramas & was nick-named "The Blood 'Tub" Anyway,it used to do a wonderful business & the place was always packed.My Dad felt very greatful to the people of Blyth for their generous support & thought it would be a nice gesture to show his appreciation by building a nice new modern theatre for their pleasure & entertainment.he thought they deserved it in return for their wonderful patronage in the past.

Well,he invested a great deal of money & the New Theatre Royal was erected,the most modern theatre of it's time - electric lighting,the floors were carpeted,tip up red velvet chairs etc. Lifts instead of stairs to the Balcony & Gallery,even had a nursery with nurses in attendance to take care of the children so the parents & others in the audience would'nt be disturbed during the performance.The orchestra were in evening dress, the Stage crew in white uniforms,also the program & chocolate boys dressed as page boys with white

2.

gloves - not a thing was spared.Believe it or not it turned
out a fiasco,the place was to elegant & the people would'nt
come in,they liked the sawdust & wooden benches much better,they
felt out of place in the beautiful surroundings,I imagine the
feeling was they would have to be dressed up instead of coming
in their weekday clothes,so the only time they did come was
Saturday night,wearing their Sunday suit!. It broke my Dad
financially so he gave it up along with his other theatres in
North Shields - Jarrow,Hebburn & Wallsend & we moved to Glasgow
where he took control of the old Metropole Theatre - was'nt
that awful? Yes,I have a memory of Blyth I shall never forget.
That was odd that you did'nt have to change in marriage name
& too that you were born right next door to where you now live,
thats certainly a coincidence. Well,think thats all for now

119

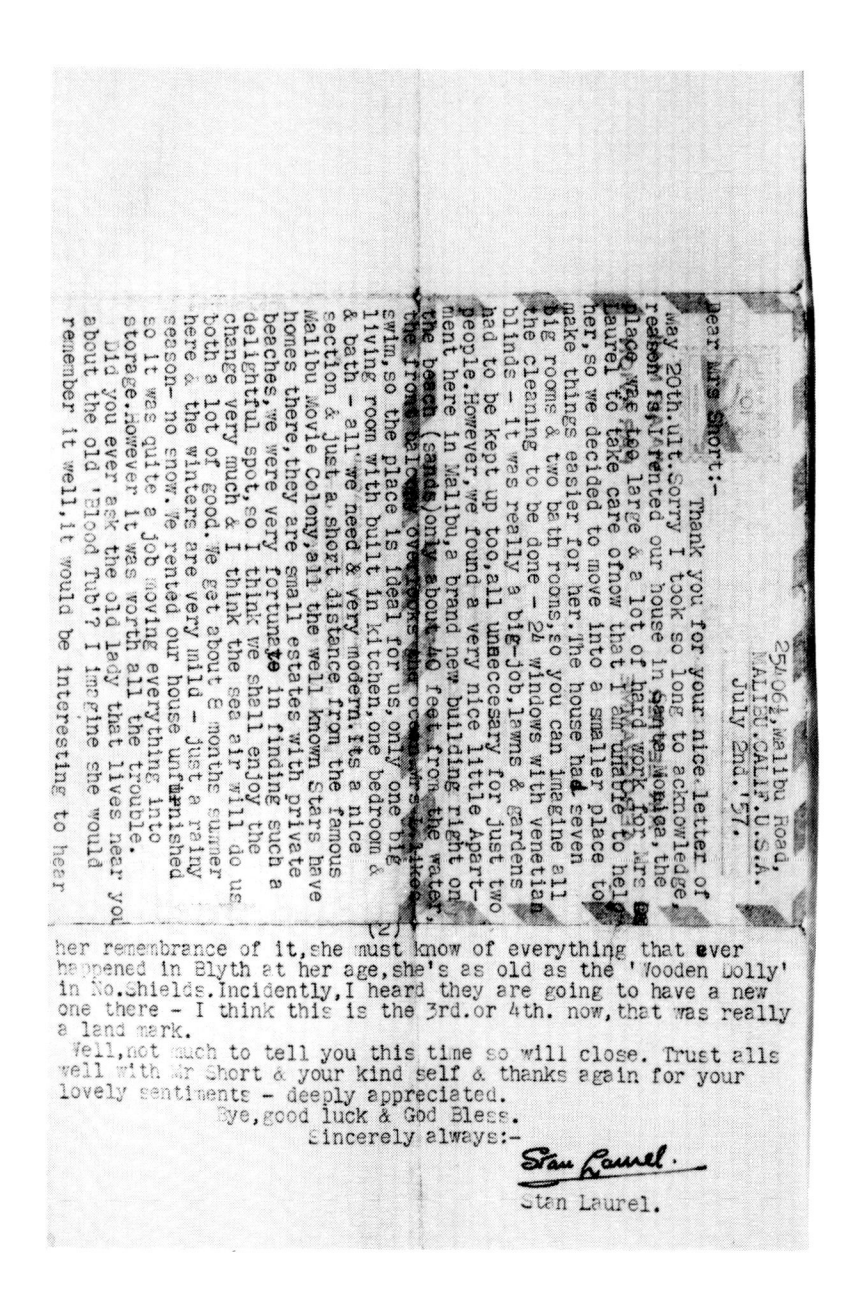

25406½ Malibu Road,
MALIBU,CALIF,U.S.A.
July 2nd.'57.

Dear Mrs Short:-

Thank you for your nice.letter of May 20th.ult.Sorry I took so long to acknowledge, reason is I rented our house in Santa,Monica, the place was too large & a lot of hard work for Mrs Laurel to take care of,now that I am unable to help her,so we decided to move into a smaller place to make things easier for her,the house had seven big rooms & two bath rooms,so you can imagine all the cleaning to be done - 24 windows with venetian blinds - it was really a big job,lawns & gardens had to be kept up too,all uneccesary for just two people.However,we found a very nice little Apart- ment here in Malibu,a brand new building right on the beach (sands)only about 40 feet from the water, the front balcony overlooks the ocean,very nice. swim,so the place is ideal for us,only one big living room with built in kitchen,one bedroom & & bath - all we need & very modern,its a nice section & just a short distance from the famous Malibu Movie Colony,all the well known Stars have homes there,they are small estates with private beaches,we were very fortunate in finding such a delightful spot,so I think we shall enjoy the change very much & I think the sea air will do us both a lot of good.We got about 8 months summer here & the winters are very mild - just a rainy season- no snow.We rented our house unfurnished so it was quite a job moving everything into storage.However it was worth all the trouble.
Did you ever ask the old lady that lives near you about the old 'Blood Tub'? I imagine she would remember it well,it would be interesting to hear

(2)

her remembrance of it,she must know of everything that ever happened in Blyth at her age,she's as old as the 'Wooden Dolly' in No.Shields.Incidently,I heard they are going to have a new one there - I think this is the 3rd.or 4th. now,that was really a land mark.
Well,not much to tell you this time so will close. Trust alls well with Mr Short & your kind self & thanks again for your lovely sentiments - deeply appreciated.
Bye,good luck & God Bless.
Sincerely always:-

Stan Laurel.

Stan Laurel.

25406½,Malibu Road,
MALIBU.CALIF.U.S.A.
July I2th.'57.

Dear Mrs Short:-

  Many thanks your very interesting letter 9th.inst. with
enclosure of the clipping regarding the new 'Wooden Dolly'.A friend of
mine just sent me some post card pictures of the new Tyne Tunnel,its
certainly a wonderful project – I told my friend,he would have to wear his
Sunday clothes everytime he went through it,its too nice to gan through in
yer bare feet!

It looks like they are really modernizing the old Tyneside,I would'nt be
surprised if the new 'Wooden Dolly' looks like Marilyn Monroe,they'll
probably have a water tank in her Creel to keep live Silver Herring!. I
imagine the old 'H'appney Dodger' (Tyne ferry) will be going out of
business & one of the discarded Navy BattleShips will be used instead.

I guess the old folks you talk to about the 'Blood Tub" get quite a kick
reminiscing over the old days,I think that show the old chap remembers
seeing last was 'The Third Alarm' (not 'Night Alarm') I saw it many times,
it was a story of a Fireman,quite a thrilling melo-drama – burning bldgs.
etc.If I remember correctly,they had a fire engine & horses come on the
stage – very spectacular.

I hope the old Lady did'nt feel insulted at my reference to her as being
as old as the Wooden Dolly,I did'nt mean to be disrespectful,it was only
in the spirit of fun – please explain that to her.

Was sorry to hear of your disappointment with the Manageress of the Theatre
Royal,I think a person running a local Cinema would be more courteous to
their patrons,she certainly shows very bad taste in treating you in that
manner,she could have at least written you a little note on returning your
letter.Anyway do'nt worry about it,she just does'nt know any better.

It was very interesting indeed to read your letter that appeared in the
Evening Chronicle,bequeathing your eyes & Bodies to the R.V.I. & Medical
school,that was certainly a wonderful gesture.Over here,people are paid
for this,hospitals will buy your body in advance & after a death will have
claim on it for research – I think I'd get about Fourpence Three Farthings
for mine,think I'll wait till prices go up!! I'm at least worth a Bob!

Well, think I'll be gaan hinney,thanks again for your kind thoughts &
wishes –enjoyed hearing from you again.

  My kind regards & best to Mr Short & self,trust alls well &
happy.

    Bye,good luck & God Bless.
    Sincerely always,

    Stan Laurel.

    Stan Laurel.

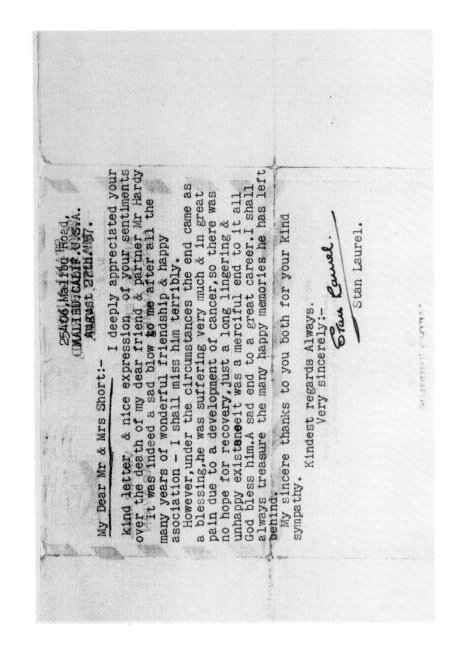

25406,Malibu Road,
MALIBU,CALIF.U.S.A.
August 27th.'57.

My Dear Mr & Mrs Short:-   I deeply appreciated your
kind letter & nice expression of your sentiments
over the death of my dear friend & partner Mr Hardy.
It was indeed a sad blow to me after all the
many years of wonderful friendship & happy
asociation - I shall miss him terribly.

However,under the circumstances the end came as
a blessing,he was suffering very much & in great
pain due to a development of cancer,so there was
no hope for recovery,just a long lingering &
unhappy existance.it was a merciful end to it all
God bless him.A sad end to a great career.I shall
always treasure the many happy memories he has left
behind.

My sincere thanks to you both for your kind
sympathy.

Kindest regards Always.
          Very sincerely:-

                              Stan Laurel.
                              —Stan Laurel.

25406,Malibu Road,
MALIBU,CALIF.U.S.A.
Jan.6th.'58.

Dear Mr & Mrs Short;-
                    Thank you for the lovely
Card.I appreciated very much your kind thought &
remembrance - very sweet of you.
  Hope you had a lovely Xmas & the New Year will
bring you lots of good health & happiness.
  I had quite a few letters & cards from my friends
on the Tyneside,you all made my Xmas very happy,
wish I could fully express the pleasure it gave
me, bless your hearts.
  I understand great changes are being made in
No.Shields.Dockwray Square where I used to live
is all being torn down to make way for new flats,
the old 'Boro' theatre that my Dad originally
built has closed for good,& they are going to
have a brand new 'Wooden Dolly', they are sure
fixing up the old Town,all the old land marks
are gradually disappearing - everybody will soon
have to wear their Sunday clothes every day.
  Weather here is very warm - like Summer,'84
degrees today,the only snow we see here is on
Television.!
          Well,all for now,trust alls well & happy.
              Good luck & God Bless you.
                  Sincerely always:-
                        Stan Laurel.

  P.S.will enjoy hearing from you anytime you
    feel like dropping a line.

25406,Malibu Road,
MALIBU.CALIF.U.S.A.
Feb.12th.'58.

My Dear Friends:-

Thanks your nice letter of Jan.30th.also for the nice picture of you both with the charming little girl,she is certainly cute. It surprised me at first,I thought she was yours.'

When I opened the letter I saw the drawing on the back of the picture & it looked like a horse collar!(the heart was upside down) - thanks for the sweet thought.

Was sorry to hear of your knee accident,must have been very painful. You should wear one of those knee supporters,made of elastic.I used to use ankle supports when I worked,they are very good protection.

You sure created a big job for yourself,copying all my letters for Dr.ivory,must have taken quite a time. Nice to know he had such an interest in L&H,its gratifying to feel that we made so many wonderful friends during our career,makes me very happy indeed.

Note you have been having unusually cold weather this year,must have put the ice cream people out of business.! They are having a great deal of snow in the Eastern States right now - how lucky I am to be in So. California.

I was shocked when I heard about that terrible plane crash with the Manchester United Football Team aboard - what a tragedy,all young lads. I enjoyed reading the items you enclosed - very interesting.

Well I'll have to be gaan now,dinner's ready - am having a Tyneside Pheasant (a kipper with a feather stuck in it.!!!).

Bye,good luck & God Bless.

Sincerely always:-

Stan Laurel.

Stan Laurel.

124

2546 Beverly Road.
Malibu. Calif. U.S.A.
April 11th.'58.

Dear Mr & Mrs Short:

Many thanks your nice letter of March
31st. also the lovely Easter Greetings Card,it was very
thoughtful of you & much appreciated.

Was so sorry to hear about the 94 year old Lady being in
Preston Hospital,I imagine little can be done for her due to
age & mental affliction,thats a sad situation poor soul.
I too was sorry to read of your dear friend being killed in
an auto accident - must have been quite a shock to you,that
was awful - just in the prime of life - never know do we.
Some friends of mine who live in Stocksfield,sent me the
enclosed news clipping,thought it might interest you - am
wonderfing if you saw this show at the Theatre Royal Blyth.?
I do'nt remember this Mr Bradley as its many years ago.Funny
thing,the article mentions that the Pantomine opened in Bishop
Auckland.(Durham) that was another of my Dads theatres which
he leased for several years - the Eden Theatre. & I used to
board at the King James Grammar School in B.A. which is still
in existence - I think I have the honour of been the worst
scholar that ever attended there.!

We too have been having lots of rain here which caused a
great deal of damage,floods & landslides,thousands of families
are homeless,the worst storms in many years.

Think thats about all for now - hope you had a happy Easter
& alls well.

Bye,good luck & God Bless.
Sincerely always:-

Stan Laurel.

25406,Malibu Road,
MALIBU.CALIF.U.S.A.
May 19th.'58.

Dear Mrs Short:

Thank you for your interesting letter of the 12th.inst.
with enclosure of news clippings. The new Power Station is quite a
big project,& should provide a lot of employment around Bedlington &
bring prosperity into the neighborhood – its wonderful to see a little
community starting to improve & grow up.

I note the Theatre Royal Blyth is trying legitimate shows again in
place of films,I imagine they should do very well if the shows have
any merit – I think the people like a change in entertainment.

Sorry to hear the weather is still bad,its beautiful here,warm &
sunny again.

Not much to tell you,except we are busy looking around for another
apartment,our lease expires June 25th.hoping to find a place in
Santa Monica so we can be closer to our few friends.This place is very
nice but a bit isolated for us as we like to have company. As soon as
I know the new address,will send it on to you.

I understand the new 'Wooden Dolly" is to be unveiled soon in North
Shields as soon as they decide on a good site – a friend of mine who
lives in Stocksfield sent me a news picture of it,the wood carvers
did a wonderful job,I believe it cost over £200. – pretty reasonable
for that kind of work.

Well,all for now.Enjoyed hearing from you again. Mrs L.joins in
Kindest regards & every good wish to Mr Short & self – take care of
yoursel Hinney.

Good luck & God Bless.   Sincerely always:– *Stan Laurel.*

849 OCEAN AVENUE
SANTA MONICA, CALIF.
Sept.25th.'59.

Dear Mrs Short:
                Thanks your nice letter,13th.inst.
Nice to hear from you again,& to know alls well & happy with
you.
        Many thanks for your kind birthday greetings – I was 69
last June.
        Yes, I was born in Ulverston,Lancs.in 1890. but left there at
an early age – lived in Bishop Auckland,Durham,a few years
then came to North Shields & went to school in Tynemouth.
        My only connection with Jarrow was,that my Dad ran the
Theatre Royal there.
        Everything with me is just as usual,so not much to tell
you,so you will have to excuse my briefness. Thanks again
for your kind thoughts & sentiments – wish you & Mr Short
continued good health & happiness.
                Sincerely always:
                        Stan Laurel.
                        Stan Laurel.

849 OCEAN AVENUE
SANTA MONICA, CALIF.
January 15.'60.

Dear Mr & Mrs Short:
                    Many thanks for the nice Card.
Appreciated very much your kind thought & remembrance.
    Hope you had a very Merry Xmas,& trust the New Year
will bring you both lots of good health,happiness &

Prosperity. Trust alls well & happy with you.
    Mrs L. joins in kindest regards.
                    Sincerely always:
                        STAN LAUREL.

MAY 15th. '61.

Many thanks your kind congratulations on my Oscar Award.- appreciate very much your kind sentiments. Am very thrilled to receive such a wonderful tribute - only wish my dear late partner could have been here to share this great honor he helped make possible.

Thanks again for your kind thoughts.

Trust alls well & happy with you.

Cheerio & God Bless.

As ever:

Stan Laurel.

STAN LAUREL.

DEC. 18th. '61.

Thanks for your kind remembrance. We here too
wish you both a very Merry Xmas, lots of good
health, success & happiness in 1962.
      Good luck – God Bless.

      Sincerely as ever:

                              Stan Laurel.
                              STAN LAUREL.

MARCH I2th. '62.

Dear Mr & Mrs Short:

Many thanks your interesting letter with enclosure of news clippings re the 'Old Theatre Royal,Blyth,& the news letter of Bert Cole a former employee in the early days,it was indeed in those days a beautiful theatre,complete in every detail a credit to any community. I hope it will be considered & converted into a Civic Auditorium,& will be spared destruction – I feel the building has historic value as a landmark & should be preserved– The Town & district need such a place to hold their local meeting & important affairs,besides establishing talent & local Culture in the future.

Pleased to know you enjoyed the old film "Dancing Masters" at the 'Tatler' in Newcastle.

Nice to hear from you again & to know alls well with you.

Nothing much exciting to tell you,so bye for now. Again,my kindest regards & every good wish,

Very sincerely:

Stan Laurel.

STAN LAUREL.

THE Oceana
APARTMENT HOTEL

849 OCEAN AVENUE, SANTA MONICA, CALIFORNIA · EXBROOK 3-0496

JUNE 6th.1962.

Dear Mr & Mrs Short:
                    Thanks your nice letter of
the 2nd.inst. Nice to hear from you again & to
know alls well & happy with you.
        Appreciate very much your kind remembrance &
birthday greetings for my 72nd.!
        Please thank your butcher Mr Stephenson for his
nice message & please give him the little picture
enclosed. Note there is a Street near the old
Theatre Royal named 'Jefferson St' - its possible
it could have been named after my Dad,he was very
well thought of in that area, but if the Street had
been built after his time,I doubt the name would
have any connection - sorry to know they have
decided to move the old 'Royal' - too bad.!
        The pianist you mention at the'Bedlington
Terrier' pub is evidently my Sister's Son - I
only met him once,he came to see me at the Empire in
Newcastle in 1947 - yes,there is a strong family
resemblance,he is the issue of my Sister's first
marriage I understand.
                    You may be interested to know
there is a book just published in England,titled
"Mr Laurel & Mrs Hardy" by John McCabe - its
published by the Museum Press,Ltd. in London,its
possible you could borrow a copy of it at your local
Public Library - hope you'll enjoy & find it
interesting.
                Mrs L.joins in kindest regards,
                Good luck - God Bless.
                As ever sincerely:

                STAN LAUREL.

JULY 12th. 1962.

Dear Mr & Mrs Short: Thanks your nice letter 9th.
Inst. The news report that I lost an eye is greatly
exaggerated, I had a hemorrhage in my left eye
few months ago which slightly affected my vision,
my Dr. advises me that in many of these cases
nature restores the eye, some take longer than others
I still have sight, but of course its weak - anyway
am not discouraged - if its was good enough for
Lord Nelson, its quite good enough for me .!!!
Again my regards & best.
         Take care - God Bless.
            As ever sincerely:

                    Stan Laurel

                    STAN LAUREL.

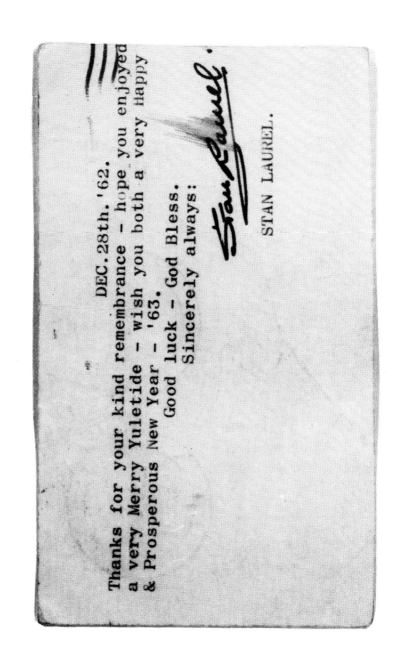

DEC. 28th. '62.

Thanks for your kind remembrance – hope you enjoyed
a very Merry Yuletide – wish you both a very happy
& Prosperous New Year – '63.

Good luck – God Bless.

Sincerely always:

Stan Laurel

STAN LAUREL.

THE Oceana
APARTMENT HOTEL

849 OCEAN AVENUE, SANTA MONICA, CALIFORNIA   EXBROOK 3-0486

AUGUST 29th.'62.

Dear Mrs Short:
                    Thanks yours,24th.inst.with
enclosure of letters from Mr Omiston,manager of the
Tatler News Theatre in Newcastle-On-Tyne. When
 you visit him again,please convey my thanks &
appreciation for his kind sentiments so graciously
expressed. Note you are going to see the L&H films
 Mr Omiston listed for the next few months,trust
they will still afford you a few laughs & happy
memories.   Am returning your letters herewith as
you requested. Again my kindest regards & every goo
wish to Mr Short & your kind self.
                    God Bless you Hinney.!
                    Sincerely always:

                    Stan Laurel

                    STAN LAUREL.

Mr & Mrs Short.

849 OCEAN AVENUE
SANTA MONICA, CALIF.

JAN.19th.'65.

My Dear Friends:
                    Thanks your letter 15th.inst.
Note you are now living in Barrington - wish you lots of
happiness in your new surroundings - your description of the house
sounds quite roomy & comfortable,am sure you will enjoy it when
you add the finishing touches & get settle down.
     Remember me kindly to Mr Ormiston (Tatler Cinema) when you see hi
again also Mr Cairn of the Tyne-Tees TV.
     I remember the little Lad you mention - they soon grow up do'nt the
I assume he has finished his schooling & possibly working by now.
     again a Happy & prosperous 1965. (from us both here.)
                    Good luck & God Bless.
                         Sincerely always:

                         STAN LAUREL.

APRIL 13th. '63.

Dear Friends: Many thanks for the nice card, the
kind thought & remembrance is much appreciated -
we here too wish you both a very Happy Easter,
continued good health & happiness. Pleased to
know you are happy in your new surroundings -
Take care - God Bless.
As always,

Stan Laurel.

STAN LAUREL.

DEC.6th. '63.

Dear Friends: Thanks your kind letter, 29th.ult.
The tragic death of our beloved president
Kennedy was indeed a sad & sickening shock - a
great great loss to the U.S.A. & the whole world
in fact - why all this HATE in the world today?
its incredibile & frightening - Mrs L. joins in
wishing you both a very Merry Xmas, continued good
health, success & happiness in '64.
Take care - God Bless you -
As always sincerely:

Stan Laurel.

STAN LAUREL.

849 OCEAN AVENUE, SANTA MONICA, CALIFORNIA · EXBROOK 3-0486

SEPT.15th.'64.

Dear Mr & Mrs Short:
                    Thanks yours,9th.inst.
with enclosure of new clipping which I am
herewith returning.
                    I had several of these
sent me also a letter from the 'Daily Express'
apologizing for the mistake - I know of this
chap,he claims his family name is Laurel &
using the name of Joe Laurel,he's a night Club
entertainer,a comic dancer or something - his wife
also works in the act with him & for some time
now he poses as my Brother.At present he is
playing in Australia. I have no idea who the little
Girl is in this picture - I do'nt think he has any
children - anyway ,I appreciate very much your
trouble. Pleased to tell you am feeling much
improved since I returned home from the hospital.
          Trust alls well & Happy with you - Mrs L
joins in kindest & bestest -
                    Take care - God Bless.
                    as always -

                    STAN LAUREL.

Chapter Sixteen
Memories

Overleaf is a treasured photograph belonging to Mr. John Marsh, who now lives in Kendal. It was taken in 1947, outside Stan Laurel's birthplace in Argyle Street, Ulverston. Mr. Marsh, then aged 15, remembered that he was out in the town doing his mother's shopping when he heard people talking about Laurel and Hardy and discovered that they were in the town that day. The crowds had gathered outside the Coronation Hall to catch a glimpse of the great comedians, but John wanted to get a closer look. "I went to Argyle Street and waited on the front door step until they arrived," he said.

There were few people outside the house as most of the crowd were following Laurel and Hardy down from the Coronation Hall, so John had a grandstand view. Oliver Hardy seemed at a bit of a loss, said John, as this was Stan's home and birthplace. "They came towards the house and Oliver Hardy said to me 'hello young man, how are you?' he recalled. On his way out of 3 Argyle Street, Stan also caught sight of young John still waiting on the doorstep. "As he came out of the house he said hello to me." said John, "they were great film stars and I was very excited to see them in real life."

The photograph appeared in the North West Evening Mail shortly after the visit of the two stars.

*Stan and Ollie outside
3 Argyle Street, back
right is the young
John Marsh.*

Chapter Seventeen

The Last Family Reunion

Mrs. Nancy Wardell was present at the last family reunion between Stan Laurel and his English cousins in 1952. She remembers it as follows. "In 1932 Laurel and Hardy came to England. Stan however was unable to make private visits to his relatives or to visit places he had been familiar with during his early life, due to his unexpected but welcome popularity. Even in their later visits to England it was difficult for Stan to have time or opportunity to move around in a private capacity. It seemed there would be no possibility of a family reunion — but a day was eventually arranged.

"One Sunday in 1952, when he was playing at a theatre for a fortnight and therefore had no need to move from one hotel to another, he spent the day with his English cousins in Yorkshire. Stan and the remaining four cousins who were all born in Ulverston had a party in Dewsbury. "A chauffeur brought Stan and his wife Ida to the Dewsbury Empire where his cousin Jack met them and took them back to his home in Woodkirk, Dewsbury. There Stan and Ida had an early lunch then went on to Nellie's home in Birkdale, Dewsbury. On the way to Nellie's house, Jack stopped the car so that Stan could see the places in Batley he had left behind when he went to America. When he arrived at Nellie's he was welcomed by Nellie, Mary and Charlie and the whole family. It was a wonderful day. Stan was able to talk, play games go into the kitchen and 'steal' cakes and generally feel at home, just for a day.

"He pretended to play the piano and all but Mary were fooled. She knew he could not play the piano and he knew she could, so her laughter was rewarded by her being made to play for him. Charlie's son played the violin very well and he was congratulated by Stan, but Stan proceeded to show him how to "sell" himself to an audience. Stan 'played' the violin, raised his eyebrows and smiled at the audience, all of which was entertaining in itself — there was no need for sound.

The cousins enjoyed each other's company along with the in-laws and the younger cousins. It was strange to realise he was so famous and at the same time was one of their family. Ida particularly, absorbed the family atmosphere, her family was in Russia and she had been unable to contact them. She was much amused by Charlie, the other family comic, whom Stan liked to call Sir Charles. In fact the family entertained Stan and Ida as much as he entertained them. Mary and her husband were excellent pianists and she was a good singer. She had been tutored when she was young by Stan's mother Madge. Charlie was extremely funny too and Stan was able to sit back and laugh at him. Nellie was the mother, she mothered them all including Stan.

"It was a day all too short. Stan and Ida had to go. The family hoped to have another re-union but sadly that did not happen. Jack took Stan and Ida back to meet their chauffeur in town and the people of Dewsbury and Batley did not know that Stan Laurel had been in their midst until after his visit. The chauffeur got lost and asked a policeman directions and Stan was recognised. The secret was out!"